AF522385

Introduction to Information Technology

Introduction to Information Technology

Shailendra Sengar

ANMOL PUBLICATIONS PVT. LTD.
NEW DELHI-110 002 (INDIA)

ANMOL PUBLICATIONS PVT. LTD.
H.O.: 4374/4B, Ansari Road, Darya Ganj,
New Delhi-110 002 (India)
Ph.: 23278000, 23261597
B.O.: No. 1015, Ist Main Road, BSK IIIrd Stage
IIIrd Phase, IIIrd Block
Bangalore - 560 085 (India)
Visit us at: www.anmolpublications.com

Introduction to Information Technology

First Published, 2008
ISBN 978-81-261-3434-2

PRINTED IN INDIA

Printed at Mehra Offset Press, Delhi.

Contents

Preface

This Encyclopaedic Series of Career and Vocational Guidance Covers careers, describing jobs, places of employment, working conditions, qualifications, education and training. This has been developed to aid career and counsellors and job placement coordinators in planning activities for students and potential students about career vocational education programs. It contains a career and vocational guidance model which clarifies what career and vocational guidance services mean and what planners should include in their activities. The model shows an interrelatedness among major thrusts with career development being a central theme of vocational guidance. All of the thrusts depicted in the model represent essential services that should be available to students in career and vocational education programs. The encyclopaedia deals with various sections which correspond to the major thrusts identified in the model: (1) career development; (2) recruitment; (3) guidance and counselling; (4) placement; (5) follow-up and follow-through; and (6) consultation. Each section contains an outline of the perceived needs of the topic, an overview of the topic relative to career and vocational guidance, and some suggested activities and strategies that may be useful in meeting student needs.

It also contains current information about occupations, employment trends, and job searching. Materials on career decision-making, internships, and salaries are also located in each volume. This Series of Encyclopaedia helps students assess their potential for various careers.

Shailendra Sengar

1

The World of Information Technology

Introduction

Information technology (IT), as defined by the Information Technology Association of America (ITAA) is: "the study, design, development, implementation, support or management of computer-based information systems, particularly software applications and computer hardware." In short, IT deals with the use of electronic computers and computer software to convert, store, protect, process, transmit and retrieve information, securely.

In this definition, the term "information" can usually be replaced by "data" without loss of meaning. Recently it has become popular to broaden the term to explicitly include the field of electronic communication so that people tend to use the abbreviation ICT (Information and Communication Technology). Strictly speaking, this name contains some redundancy.

The World has entered the new millennium, which is going to be an Information Technology Age. Today Computers have not only assumed strategic importance in the corporate world, they are being effectively used in other fields ranging from space exploration to food processing and banking to communication etc.

In this era of Information Technology, which has revolutionised the whole world, INDIA has stood to the world standards and is being regarded the World over for it's skilled

IT Professionals. Even the government has recognised the promising future of this industry and has formed a new IT Ministry which will give a boost to this industry.

Presence of Multinationals like IBM, HP has made possible transfer of hardware technology into the country, Internet has further bridged the time gap ensuring arrival of the latest technology simultaneously in INDIA and the West without delay. The domestic hardware industry has witnessed quantum growth in the turnover and profits, which is largely attributable to our liberalized economy. On the software front various software giants like IBM, Motorola, Oracle, Samsung, HP, Digital, Unisys, AT&T, ICL, Fugitsu, etc. have opened software development centres in the country.

The number of professionals in this industry is believed to have crossed the 2 lakh mark and still there is a huge gap between the demand and supply of professionals which is an encouraging sign. The US alone requires around 3 lakh professionals, leave aside other countries. It is believed around 65% of the world's software is produced in INDIA. INDIA is also exporting software to around 100 countries including many countries which are exclusive buyers from INDIA. Many Indian IT companies like Infosys, Wipro, NIIT, Zenith computers, Satyam Computers, STG, Pentafore Software, Mastek etc. are expanding themselves in a big way making their presence felt globally.

The phenomenal growth which this industry is witnessing has lead to it being recognised as one of the highly paid industry. As this industry is young, the average age of professionals is lower than any other industry. The availability of skilled, qualified professionals is hardly able to meet the requirement, leaving a large gap to be filled by those with ambition, aptitude and willingness to work hard.

Nature of Work: Following are the career areas in this industry.

1. *Software:* Software is a set of programmed instructions that enable the computer to perform specified functions. This industry offers vast range of employment opportunities in fields starting from data entry, computer

operations, programming, system analysis to system designing, system engineering and operation management. Today, this industry is one of the most sought after industry as far as returns are concerned.

2. *Hardware:* Hardware denotes the physical components of a computer. The key areas which can be taken up as career includes hardware designing, research and development, assembling, manufacturing and maintenance of computer components.
3. *Telecom:* Telecommunications is a growing industry and has created ample of scope for people joining telecommunication engineering. The various fields which can be pursued as career in this industry include voice processing units, telephone technology, wireless technology, cellular technology, touchtone telephones, microwave and satellite communication systems.
4. *Sales & Marketing:* Sales and marketing in IT industry is a specialist task and requires a thorough study of products and their competition. Marketing covers selling of both hardware and software products. This job is both competetive and challenging but not difficult as the demand for hardware and software is quite high and does not require much effort in fixing a deal.
5. *E-commerce and Web Development:* The coming together of computers and telecommunication technologies has led to the emergence of electronic commerce. Marketing and banking activities have already started taking place worldwide through Internet generating an Internet economy. Most of the future jobs anticipated in IT industry will be Internet related. These will include consumer/buyer information and services, developing and managing Web-portals, creation of Internet market, customer management, consulting etc.
6. *Enterprise Resource Planning:* ERP is planning the resources of entire network of an enterprise. Various fields like purchase, production, marketing, distribution, sales, service, inventory, finance, accounts, human resource are integrated on a single software through

ERP, to facilitate better coordination. Professionals with engineering background in mechanical, civil, manufacturing, textile as well as MBAs, chartered accountants, cost accountants can join technical ERP.

7. *Computer Operator:* A computer operator's job is to run both the computer and its peripheral equipment. The job may vary depending upon size of the organisation and its exposure to computers. An operator usually works on instructions issued by programmers or operation managers. Upon acquiring programming training, he can even end up being a full time efficient application programmer.
8. *Data Entry*: Data entry is transferring information into the computer and is the most basic purpose for which computers are used. Data entry operators are needed in almost every organisation using computers. People with good typing skills are best suited for these jobs.

What Careers Will I Qualify For With an Information Technology Degree?

"Information technology jobs lie within one of four main career paths. The broad Computer Science Application grouping includes systems analysts, computer programmers, computer scientists, software engineers and database/network administrators. The remaining positions fall under either the Management/Supervisory group (*e.g.*, project or technical managers), in Customer Service and Support (computer support specialists), or in Sales/Relationship Management (sales engineers)."

Possible Job Titles for Associate's or Bachelor's IT Degree Holders / Entry Level Job Titles.

Here is a sampling of jobs you for which you may be qualified with a degree in Information Technology. Use this for inspiration, remembering that this may represents some, but certainly not all, of the careers you can consider.

- Application Developer
- Business Analyst
- Computer Service Technician

- Database Analyst
- Database Developer
- Help Desk Analyst
- IT Business Analyst
- IT Specialist
- SQL Server DBA
- Junior .ASP Developer
- Junior .NET Developer
- Network Systems Analyst
- Project Manager
- Technical Analyst
- Software Tester
- Industrial Designer
- User Interface Designer
- Web Metrics Analyst
- Web-Internet Developer
- Wireless Support Analyst

Possible Job Titles for Advanced IT Degree Holders:

- Chief Information Officer
- Computer Engineer
- C++/UNIX Software Engineer
- Data Processing Manager
- Database Administrator
- Hardware Engineer
- Industrial Designer
- Information Architect
- Instructional Technology Manager
- .NET C# Developer
- Network Administrator
- Oracle Developer
- QA Engineer
- Robotics Engineer
- Senior Information Technology Engineer

- JAVA/J2EE Developer
- Software Developer
- Systems Consultant
- Systems Manager
- Telecommunications Engineer

Information Technology

These days, it seems as if everything is controlled by computers. Not in a bad way, of course: Stanley Kubrick's worst fears as witnessed by *2001: A Space Odyssey* won't be coming true anytime soon. But the fact remains that from the databases maintained by the IRS to the purchasing records of supermarkets to the information doctors keep of their patients, computers have become the single essential tie that binds the world together. It therefore should come as no surprise that a degree in information technology is more marketable now than it ever has been in the past.

Information technology "is the study, design, development, implementation and support of computer-based information systems to address real -world problems". In other words, it is the science (and, indeed, some might even say the art) of working with computers in order to facilitate the easier and more efficient use of them by non-professionals and professionals alike.

Niche Areas: As has been noted several times already, there are many specific areas of the IT field on which you may choose to focus. They include, but are not limited to, the following:

- Graphics and Imaging
- Operating Systems
- Personal Information Management
- Publishing
- Document Management
- Statistical Analysis & Mathematical Modelling
- Document Integration
- Administrative Systems

Types of Associate, Undergraduate & Graduate Programmes Available: Over the course of the past decade, more and more colleges and universities have begun offering degree programmes in information technology. This is because of the ever-increasing importance of the skill-sets IT practitioners possess. An associate's degree in IT will prepare you for further study at the undergraduate level, as well as provide an adequate base of knowledge that you may attempt to parlay to a job as an entry-level programmer or database manager.

A bachelor's degree in IT affords you the opportunity to learn about all aspects of the field and to begin the process of narrowing down your areas of specific interest so that you can attain a certain amount of expertise. Graduate degrees in IT are generally either for those who wish to pursue collegiate teaching or research, or who wish to eventually work in the highest levels of the technology world—government computer development or computer and software design, for example.

Typical Admissions Requirements: Getting into an associate's degree programme in IT is not terribly difficult at all. As long as you have an interest in the field and a bit of previous experience with computers, then you should be fine. At the higher levels of education in the IT field, however, competition can become rather stiff.

Indeed, because of the high skill level of many applicants and the popularity of the field in general, there are likely to be many people with high levels of ability vying for a small number of spots. Don't let that discourage you, however. If you are truly interested in the field and even if you don't get in the first time you try, you should not throw in the towel. Perhaps with a bit of work experience and a bit of additional effort, you, too, will be on your way to a degree in information technology.

Careers in This Field: Because of the many and wide-ranging applications of computers and software, there is a nearly infinite variety of career options available to graduates of IT programmes. They include, but are not limited to, the following:

- Computer Software Engineer, Systems Software
- Computer Systems Analysts
- Computer Support Specialists
- Computer Programmers
- Computer and Information Systems Managers
- Computer Software Engineers, Applications
- Database Administrators
- Computer Security Specialists
- Computer and Information Scientists, Research

Salary Ranges in this Field: Because of the wide variety of careers available to those possessing degrees in IT, it is difficult to narrow down how much they stand to make. A government employee, for example, may very well make less money than an IT expert working with, say, a publicly-held financial institution on Wall Street. Also affecting the amount of money you stand to eventually make is the specific area of IT on which you choose to focus. Therefore, in order to more fully and accurately gauge what you'll eventually earn, it is best to do research on as specific an area as possible in the IT field.

Future Outlook: Because the IT field is so large and wide-ranging, it is virtually impossible to discuss the job outlook in general terms. However, the field of computer and information systems managers is as good a place to begin as any and the outlook for it is likely indicative of larger trends in the field. According to the United States Bureau of Labour Statistics:

"Employment of computer and information systems managers is expected to grow faster than the average for all occupations through the year 2014. Technological advancements will boost the employment of computer-related workers; as a result, the demand for managers to direct these workers also will increase. In addition, job openings will result from the need to replace managers who retire or move into other occupations.

Opportunities for obtaining a management position will be best for those with computer-related work experience; an MBA with technology as a core component, or a management information systems degree; and strong communication and administrative skills.

Despite the downturn in the technology sector in the early part of the decade, the outlook for computer and information systems managers remains strong. To remain competitive, firms will continue to install sophisticated computer networks and set up more complex Internet and intranet sites. Keeping a computer network running smoothly is essential to almost every organization. Firms will be more willing to hire managers who can accomplish that.

Similarly, the security of computer networks will continue to increase in importance as more business is conducted over the Internet. The security of the Nation's entire electronic infrastructure has come under renewed scrutiny in light of recent threats. Organizations need to understand how their systems are vulnerable and how to protect their infrastructure and Internet sites from hackers, viruses and other acts of cyber-terrorism. The emergence of cybersecurity as a key issue facing most organizations should lead to strong growth for computer managers. Firms will increasingly hire cybersecurity experts to fill key leadership roles in their information technology departments because the integrity of their computing environments is of utmost concern. As a result, there will be a high demand for managers proficient in computer security issues.

With the explosive growth of electronic commerce and the capacity of the Internet to create new relationships with customers, the role of computer and information systems managers will continue to evolve. Persons in these jobs will become increasingly vital to their companies. The expansion of the wireless Internet will spur the need for computer and information systems managers with both business savvy and technical proficiency."

History of Information Technology

The term "information technology" came about in the 1970s. Its basic concept, however, can be traced back even further. Throughout the 20th century, an alliance between the military and various industries has existed in the development of electronics, computers and information theory. The military has historically driven such research by providing motivation and funding for innovation in the field of mechanization and computing.

The first commercial computer was the UNIVAC I. It was designed by J. Presper Eckert and John Mauchly for the U.S. Census Bureau. The late 70s saw the rise of microcomputers, followed closely by IBM's personal computer in 1981. Since then, four generations of computers have evolved. Each generation represented a step that was characterized by hardware of decreased size and increased capabilities. The first generation used vacuum tubes, the second transistors and the third integrated circuits. The fourth (and current) generation uses more complex systems such as Very-large-scale integration or System-on-a-chip.

Information Technology Today

Today, the term Information Technology has ballooned to encompass many aspects of computing and technology and the term is more recognizable than ever before. The Information Technology umbrella can be quite large, covering many fields. IT professionals perform a variety of duties that range from installing applications to designing complex computer networks and information databases. A few of the duties that IT professionals perform may include;

- Data Management
- Computer Networking
- Database Systems Design
- Software design
- Management Information Systems
- Systems management

A more extensive list of related topics is provided below.

Information Technology Title

The Commonwealth of Pennsylvania has made a substantial investment in information technology resources. Many state agencies have installed a mainframe computer, midrange computer and a local area network. Our computer systems and programming languages are continuously being evaluated and updated. Also, information technology specialists receive training in the latest technological advances.

State agencies have developed several dynamic and innovative training programmes to introduce new employees to their systems. Classroom training, specialized workshops and vendor courses form the core of the training. Employees have the opportunity to follow a progressive career path that can lead to higher levels of computer programming or computer systems analysis and management.

Many of the latest concepts in the computer field are under development or nearing implementation including integrated communications networks, client server technology, distributed technology, imaging technology, CASE tools, computer assisted design, artificial intelligence and geographic information systems. Pennsylvania state government has also been recognized as a national leader in its' management of the Year 2000 date modification. In addition, the Commonwealth is committed to providing information to the residents of Pennsylvania by utilizing the technological opportunities available through the Internet.

Information technology (IT) is a label that has two meanings. In common usage, the term "information technology" is often used to refer to all of computing. As a name of an undergraduate degree programme, it refers to the preparation of students to meet the computer technology needs of business, government, healthcare, schools and other kinds of organizations.

IT professionals possess the right combination of knowledge and practical, hands-on expertise to take care of both an organization's information technology infrastructure and the people who use it. They assume responsibility for selecting hardware and software products appropriate for an organization. They integrate those products with organizational needs and infrastructure and install, customize and maintain those applications, so providing a secure and effective environment that supports the activities of the organization's computer users. In IT, programming often involves writing short programmes that typically connect existing components (scripting).

The shaded area extends down most of the right edge as it focuses on the application, deployment and configuration needs of organizations and people over a wide spectrum. Across this range (from organizational information systems, to application technologies and down to systems infrastructure), the role of the IT specialists has some overlap with IS, but IT people have a special focus on satisfying human needs that arise from computing technology. In addition, the IT shaded area goes leftwards from application towards theory and innovation, especially in the area of application technologies. This is because IT people often develop the web-enabled digital technologies that organizations use for a broad mix of informational purposes. This implies an appropriate conceptual foundation in relevant principles and theory.

Honeywell Technology Solutions Lab

Career: Information Technology in the Honeywell Technology Solutions Lab (HTSL) consists of developing enterprise middleware/Internet technology solutions and applications for various Honeywell businesses worldwide. The group provides value by developing solutions that result in increased productivity—mainly in custom web application development, web interface, legacy applications, enterprise application integration and information portals.

Honeywell gives motivated employees increased responsibilities. We consciously identify and develop employees from within to grow into tomorrow's leaders and managers. As a result, the typical employee enjoys a career with exponential growth, fuelled by motivation, capabilities and a desire to excel.

Honeywell Technology Solutions Lab, Honeywell's key regional arm of excellence, has operations in Bangalore and Madurai, India; Shanghai and Beijing, China; Minneapolis, Minnesota and Phoenix, Arizona, USA; Singapore; and Brno in the Czech Republic. The Bangalore-based engineering and technology lab continuously enhances expertise in mission-critical technologies in the aerospace and controls domain.

The engineering and technology lab in Bangalore has more than 3,000 employees with world-class facilities with state-of the-art hardware, software and communication infrastructure.

Career Focus: A career in Information Technology with a focus in Corporate Honeywell Technology Solutions Lab (HTSL) is an area integral to Honeywell. HTSL provides technology, product and business solutions while meeting global standards of quality, innovation and lifetime performance. Some of the applications include real-time process control, embedded real-time systems, system software and engineering tools. Research teams explore advanced technologies and frontiers in software to support Honeywell units worldwide and develop new technology-based products.

The engineering services initiative aims to provide best-in-class product and component analysis, design and prototyping in mechanical engineering and total engineering capability in electronics hardware.

HTSL is ISO 9001 TickIT certified and operates at a SEI-CMM Level 5 maturity with robust systems in place. It uses Six Sigma and Design for Six Sigma (DFSS) techniques to improve output in all areas. It recently earned PCMM Maturity Level 5 and was voted as one of the Top 10 Great Places to Work in a survey conducted by The Great Place to Work Institute, USA and Business in 2004.

Career Path: Career paths within the Honeywell Technology Solutions Lab vary greatly. Engineers with graduate, postgraduate, doctoral, or management educational qualifications join HTSL as individual contributors in the software programming, testing, research & development, or analytics business units. After gaining considerable experience and having a favourable performance rating, they can choose to go into a leadership role for technology, people, or process within their respective domains. From there, they can continue to grow. Successful leaders and experts can ultimately become strategic leaders and chief engineers.

Individuals may also move horizontally across roles. People who are currently in the role of leaders can also start afresh as individual contributors in a new technical area, domain, or function. One example is of a Mechanical Engineer at the Indian Institute of Technology. He began his career as a Software Development Engineer in the Home & Building Controls

(H&BC) business for Automation & Control Solutions (ACS). Within two years, he started leading a team of development engineers and later began leading entire project teams. His overall technical expertise in business and people management skills allowed him to become the head of the H&BC business that culminated in leading the entire ACS business unit at HTSL.

Information Technology: As it is

Size and scope: The IT workforce is almost 1.2 million strong. The sector is divided into two parts:

- those working in the IT industry;
- IT professionals working in other areas.

Inside: There are almost 580,000 people working in companies in the UK whose primary function and business is IT; this accounts for approximately 2% of UK employment.

IT professionals typically fill roles in:

- IT services (*e.g.*, internet and web design services);
- technology development;
- systems analysis and testing;
- programming.

Just under a third of those working inside the industry are employed in other, less technical occupations, for example in:

- sales and marketing;
- consultancy;
- customer support;
- management.

Outside: There are almost 590,000 IT professionals working in other sectors in the UK. These are people whose primary role is IT orientated – they often work in IT departments or as IT support staff within organisations.

Outside the IT industry, the largest numbers of IT professionals can be found in manufacturing, financial services, retail and the public sector, although there are opportunities in just about every sector. Areas of work include:

- development (*i.e.*, creating systems, networks and applications);

- operations (*i.e.*, running and improving the speed of access to systems, networks and applications);
- user support.

Employment Trends: Four out of ten UK businesses employ IT professionals. Levels of employment in specific IT roles can be distributed as follows:

Employment levels in IT Q2 2005

IT/Telecoms managers	32%
Technical support staff	28%
PC support staff	9%
Systems designers	7%
Systems developers	6%
Programmers	5%
Software engineers	5%
Operations staff	3%
Networking staff	3%
Internet professionals	2%
Database staff	1%

(*ICT Inquiry issue 3—Q2*, e-skills UK, 2005)

Location: London and the South East continue to dominate employment in IT with around 40% of IT professionals working in these two regions; Northern Ireland, Wales and Scotland account for 11% of IT employment in the UK. (*Labour Force Survey*, Office for National Statistics, 2004)

Graduate Recruitment: The number of IT jobs advertised in 2004 fell from the previous two years. However, there is substantial evidence to suggest this trend has begun to change for the period 2005-2006.

Salaries compare well. The average graduate starting salary in 2005 was £28,095. Salaries were higher again for IT jobs in large organisations. (*TARGET Graduate Trends Survey 2005/6: IT sector*, GTI Specialist Publishers, 2006)

IT professionals tend to be better qualified than the general workforce, with more than half having completed some form of higher education. According to what do graduates do? 2006, based on a national survey conducted six months after graduation, 40% of those who graduated with an IT-related degree in 2004 were working as IT professionals.

The most common roles for all new graduates are:

- software engineer;
- computer/IT consultant;
- computer programmer;
- systems analyst;
- computer analyst/programmer;
- computer operations manager.

Graduate Perceptions: Comments from graduates about what they enjoy most about working in IT reinforce perceptions of a dynamic industry that is often informal, but always focused on achievement. Highlights include:

- constant challenges and changes;
- enormous variety of work;
- relaxed work environment;
- culture of delivery and getting things done;
- part of a forever evolving and fast-moving industry;
- enthusiasm and intelligence of colleagues;
- good work/life balance.

This final point is significant as IT often has a 'long hours culture'. The cyclical nature of projects means that extra work may indeed be necessary to meet project deadlines or to provide 24/7 support; in some areas, notably the games industry, long hours are pretty much the norm. On the whole though, case studies show that many graduates work a fairly standard day.

Culture

Gender: Women form less than 20% (one in five) of the IT workforce, which is significantly low in comparison with the 45% of the UK workforce overall. Women do, however, have a higher presence in operations and user support technician roles. (*Quarterly Review of the ICT Labour Market Issue 14—Q3*, e-skills UK, 2005)

Training: The IT industry invests significantly more in training than the average invested by all other industries. This often includes training in new technology. The type of training offered will depend on the business priority of the organisation; there is tremendous diversity between companies in different areas of the sector. The following analysis of business priorities is from e-skills UK:

- IT services: customer satisfaction: revenue and profit; competitiveness; services development.
- Software product development: speed to market; product differentiation; cost control; long-term product profitability.
- IT sales and marketing: revenue; market share; win rate; customer retention.
- In-house IT: service levels and availability; cost effectiveness; systems strategy.

Skills: The industry tends to favour proven experience and ability over education and qualifications. In some roles, non-IT graduates compete with IT graduates based on the skills they have to offer, including technical and analytical skills and not necessarily degree subject studied. When recruiting for roles, almost 65% of employers seek graduates from any degree discipline. (*TARGET Graduate Trends Survey 2005/6: IT sector*, GTI Specialist Publishers, 2006)

Gaps: There is, at present, a significant IT skills gap in the UK. The British Computer Society states that current graduates do not have the technical skills the industry needs. Skills required by programmers and application developers, such as Java, are particularly lacking. This skills gap has resulted in the delay by some companies of the development of new products and services.

This is reinforced in *IT Insights: Trends and UK Skills Implications* (e-skills UK/Gartner Consulting, 2004). The report further suggests that the educational infrastructure needed to meet future skills requirements is not yet in place and the number of those applying and being accepted onto IT-related higher education courses is in decline.

Current Trends: Perhaps the most significant influences on the industry at the moment are:

- outsourcing—the concept of taking internal company functions and paying an outside firm to handle them;
- off shoring—the relocation of IT services to a lower cost location, usually overseas.

According to a recent survey by Capgemini, the UK currently outsources around 8% of its operations overseas, compared with the European average of 2%. This figure is growing annually. (*European CIO Survey: Views on Future IT Delivery*, Capgemini, 2006)

The UK has been slower and less aggressive in adopting and exploiting technology than other leading countries; businesses have failed to invest in IT, preferring to outsource instead. However, as the relationship between business productivity and company investment in IT becomes more apparent, there has been a drive towards greater IT innovation and investment. Business projects without IT as a major component are rare; companies are likely to spend more on new IT systems to inform their strategic planning and to implement business goals.

The introduction of ID cards continues to be a current and problematic issue for the UK government; it is its biggest technological challenge to date, along with developing the extensive IT structures required to make the 2012 London Olympics a success.

Graduate Careers in Information Technology (IT)

The future for students wishing to pursue a graduate career in information technology provided they develop the skills in most demand in the workplace. According to a recent survey of 5,000 staff by the Association of Technology Staffing Companies, salaries for IT staff have risen an average of 15% over the last year due to increasing demand for senior project managers and business analysts. There has never been a better time to embark on a graduate career in IT as demand for management information systems, IT managers, business systems analysts and project managers is rising dramatically.

A graduate career in IT will require you to use a variety of skills in addition to those acquired in your degree.

IT touches more areas of business than almost any other discipline. In today's business world many companies are interested in recruiting well-rounded staff who have business focused skills and can demonstrate an understanding of how IT can benefit the business as a whole and an understanding of how implementation of IT systems will impact on the organisation. People skills, self management and an ability to see IT as a means to an end, rather than an end in itself are all equally important as the traditional core IT skills.

There are currently several routes to a career in the UK IT industry including full time study, part-time study whilst in employment and on the job training. The following are just some of the options open to those interested in an IT career:

Graduation with a non-IT related subject.

An accredited degree.

Training in a specific IT skill which is in demand.

Transfer to an IT department within a company.

A year in industry/gap year experience prior to University.

Many companies are happy to recruit graduates with non IT related subjects who are willing to undertake additional IT specific training through postgraduate or professional training courses such as those offered by Information Systems Examination Board (ISEB)–a BCS subsidiary, which offers qualifications in systems analysis and design and project management, among others. It is also worth considering undertaking a language; the IT profession is global and having additional language skills can be useful in gaining employment.

For students interested in a "client facing role" a more business orientated degree such as one in finance, management or another engineering subject may prove a better grounding than a pure IT degree, providing students with a good insight into business and a better understanding of the sort of problems their future client's are likely to face.

Whichever option taken, the key to improving the chances of being recruited is to achieve the best degree possible and take advantage of any work experience offered as part of the course or during the vacations.

The most direct route into the more traditional "hard" IT roles such as software development, infrastructure and research posts, is a degree in computing followed by an application to a graduate recruitment programme.

An accredited degree offers a core of studies seen as the minimum necessary for the foundation of a professional career in the industry, together with specialist content in one or more areas studied in-depth; it will include an appropriate mix of engineering principles, design and problem-solving and practical work. BCS accredits honours degrees in the IT area for Chartered Engineer (CEng) status and professional membership. BCS also accredits degrees for Chartered Scientist. In addition, there are four-year MEng courses.

Many degree courses include a year spent in industrial training in a company with a computing environment prior to the final year. Some employers will offer sponsorship for the final year after a successful placement, with or without a guarantee of employment on graduating. After study, there are opportunities to join a graduate development programmes offered by companies for new graduates aiming to work in IT. Alternatively, graduates with a good class degree may consider studying for a PhD or moving into industrial research.

A specific training course in a skill which is in demand offers a quick way to enter the industry. Internet website design and enterprise resource planning (ERP) are just two examples of skills currently in high demand, although the market is continually changing. However, as demand for particular skills can be short-term, it is advisable to continue developing additional skills and gain broad experience.

Organizations such as Microsoft (for Windows), Novell (for networking) and Oracle (for databases) offer vendor certification courses. The Information Systems Examination Board (ISEB) offers qualifications in systems analysis and design and project management and learning can be done via classes, computer-based training or distance learning.

Courses like these which focus on specific computer skills are aimed at the experienced practitioner and are not suitable for the beginner.

Finally the European computer driving licence (ECDL) is a users' qualification recognised across the world and offers a starting point and evidence that students are prepared to train and build skills.

For information relating to skills required for each specific role in graduate careers in IT, the Skills Framework for the Information Age (SFIA), the high level UK Government backed competency framework, describes the roles within IT and the skills needed to fulfil them.

SFIAplus contains the SFIA framework of IT skills plus detailed training and development resources to provide the most established and widely adopted IT skills, training and development model reflecting current industry needs. If you are interested in pursuing a graduate career in IT, then don't delay, start enhancing your knowledge and skills with additional courses and qualifications to give your career the best possible start.

Technology, Telecoms and Contact Centres

Over the last few years, these industries have been among the fastest growing and developing sectors in the country. They have an impact on all industries.

- About two per cent of all Scottish jobs are in the IT and telecoms industries. (48,700)
- There are also IT professionals employed in other sectors; over half a million in the UK.
- The UK is the third largest telecoms market in the world.
- There are 56,000 contact centre jobs in Scotland; almost 86 per cent of these are in the central belt of Scotland.
- Most industries have contact centres; financial services, with 30 per cent of the total number of jobs, remains the most important user of contact centres.

Areas Included: The IT and telecommunications sector is responsible for:

- the installation and maintenance of communication networks
- the installation and support for new computer software and hardware

These industries have changed the way we lead our lives and altered the way in which business is conducted; you can play videos on mobile phones and hold face to face meetings with business colleagues in other countries.

There is almost no aspect of our lives that is not affected by this industry.

In Contact Centres, staff no longer just use a telephone; they also use the Internet, e-mail and SMS messaging.

- More than half of all jobs are both professionals and associate professionals.
- The most common IT professional job role in the UK is "software engineer".
- Contact Centre staff require high levels of technical, language and personal skills.

For a full list of jobs in this industry see below.

What's it like to work in the information technology, telecommunications & contact centres industry

- This industry will appeal most to those with an interest in technical work.
- Most jobs are full time – 86%.
- Most employees are men – 62%.
- Self employment in IT is slightly higher than the average.
- The average age of a worker is 36 – younger than the average of 40 for Scotland as a whole.
- In contact centres, three fifths of the workforce is female (61%).
- The prospects for graduates are good. In the last two to three years, one in four employers had recruited a graduate.

- Employers are less likely to recruit school leavers. Less than one in ten employers have recruited a school leaver in the last two to three years.

Future Trends

- Employment is expected to increase by more than 20% in the next ten years.
- Future skills shortages are expected to be in systems integration, networking and business analysis.
- Despite some call centres moving overseas and changes in technology; the industry is predicted to continue to grow.

Information Technology Jobs

At Argonne, we are building a cutting-edge computing environment enabling scientific breakthroughs and supporting laboratory business. We are looking for top-quality, highly motivated people who seek personal and professional fulfilment in their careers. Your problem-solving and leadership skills as well as a commitment to continuous improvement and customer satisfaction are needed.

Argonne is known throughout the world for leading-edge science and technology research. Argonne's future depends on high-caliber people who contribute to every aspect of the organization. Argonne is a challenging and rewarding career choice, a workplace of which we can all be proud.

Current Openings

Web Developer: As a member of the Computing and Information Systems Division, this position develops and supports web-based applications for Argonne‘s business systems and public web pages. This person will work with users across the Laboratory to analyze their requirements, define projects and implement or customize web-based applications.

Linux System Administrator: As a member of the Computing and Information Systems Division, this position implements, enhances and maintains robust, redundant, Unix-based web infrastructure and services. This person develops, implements and supports web-enabled tools for distributed Unix systems administration and participates in the conceptualization, planning and implementation of Laboratory-wide distributed UNIX computing infrastructure.

Senior Software Developer: As a member of the Leadership Computing Facility (LCF), this position builds computational tools and develops methods for the solution of computational science problems on parallel and distributed computers.

Senior Systems Administrator: As a member of the Mathematics and Computer Science Division's High-Performance Computing (HPC) team, this position is dedicated to the technical operation, support and development of the Transportation Research and Analysis Computer Center (TRACC). Special emphasis is given to leading efforts in building and maintaining systems and clusters, creating technical documentation for end-users and internal use and providing technical support to the users of HPC resources. This position is stationed at Dupage Technology Park.

Senior Software Developer: The Mathematics and Computer Science Division has two openings for senior software developers who will work with members of the Radix Laboratory, which develops software for petascale systems. They will be responsible for designing, implementing, debugging and testing new components.

Candidates should have considerable experience with Linux, computer science, software engineering and the C programming language. Familiarity with parallel programming, high-performance computing, operating systems, high-performance networking and MPI is highly desired. The appointees will work as part of an integrated, multi-institution research team whose focus extends from the investigation of algorithms to parallel scientific simulations.

Computational Scientist: As a member of the Leadership Computing Facility (LCF), this position assists and collaborates with Leadership Science Project Teams to enable breakthrough science and engineering research.

You will need comprehensive knowledge of high-performance computational science in one or more of these fields: computational materials science, computational biology, computational lattice quantum chromo dynamics and/or computational astrophysics. Also required are considerable skills in verbal and written communications, collaboration, leadership in interdisciplinary research and the solution of computational science problems using scalable parallel computers and large data systems.

Manager, Facility Operations and Networking: As a member of the Leadership Computing Facility (LCF), this position is responsible for operation of the LCF computing, storage and network hardware systems. This position requires comprehensive skills in leading system support efforts; deploying and operating advanced computing systems; and developing effective operations processes. Also required is comprehensive experience in supercomputing systems administration, including configuration, installation, monitoring and load optimization, leading to a robust and stable computing environment.

Manager, Systems Software and Integration: As a member of the Leadership Computing Facility (LCF), this position leads the team responsible for the operation of the high-performance data storage disk and tape systems and the integration of new experimental systems software on the production systems. Comprehensive knowledge of high-performance systems software and data storage systems is required, along with demonstrated organizational and communications skills and flexibility in coordinating a spectrum of activities. Experience in national facility team leadership is highly desired

Content Management Administrator: The Computing and Information Systems Division is seeking a Content Management Administrator to be part of the newly formed Web Services team to manage, customize and support the Stellent content management system.

The Web Services team is responsible for designing, creating and managing web systems and content management systems that support the Laboratory.

The ideal candidate will have strong technical skills in web technologies and collaboration tools and content management systems. Considerable experience with web development—Java, JSP, Scripting Languages, Portlets, Web Services, HTML, XML.

Optical Network Design Specialist: The Computing and Information Systems Division is seeking an optical network design specialist who will be responsible for planning, implementing, operating and testing complex optical transmission systems.

Work will include advanced fiber-optic, digital and optical cross-connect and network management systems as well as transport customer interconnect facilities. Responsibilities include system architecture and design, engineering specifications, installation and as-built documentation and verification and system monitoring methodologies.

The ideal candidate will be able to work independently with limited guidance and balance day-to-day operational needs with long-term project goals.

Jobs in Information Technology: If you are looking for some information about a specific type of job or are just curious about other career paths, review the following positions to help choose the right one for you.

Business Teachers, Postsecondary: Teach courses in business administration and management, such as accounting, finance, human resources, labour relations, marketing and operations research.

Computer and Information Scientists, Research: Conduct research into fundamental computer and information science as theorists, designers, or inventors. Solve or develop solutions to problems in the field of computer hardware and software.

Computer Hardware Engineers: Research, design, develop and test computer or computer-related equipment for commercial, industrial, military, or scientific use. May supervise the manufacturing and installation of computer or computer-related equipment and components.

Computer Operators: Monitor and control electronic computer and peripheral electronic data processing equipment to process business, scientific, engineering and other data according to operating instructions. May enter commands at a computer terminal and set controls on computer and peripheral devices. Monitor and respond to operating and error messages.

Computer Programmers: Convert project specifications and statements of problems and procedures to detailed logical flow charts for coding into computer language. Develop and write computer programmes to store, locate and retrieve specific documents, data and information. May programme web sites.

Computer Science Teachers, Post-secondary: Teach courses in computer science. May specialize in a field of computer science, such as the design and function of computers or operations and research analysis.

Computer Software Engineers, Applications: Develop, create and modify general computer applications software or specialized utility programmes. Analyze user needs and develop software solutions. Design software or customize software for client use with the aim of optimizing operational efficiency. May analyze and design databases within an application area, working individually or coordinating database development as part of a team.

Computer Software Engineers, Systems Software: Research, design, develop and test operating systems-level software, compilers and network distribution software for medical, industrial, military, communications, aerospace, business, scientific and general computing applications. Set operational specifications and formulate and analyze software requirements. Apply principles and techniques of computer science, engineering and mathematical analysis.

Computer Support Specialists: Provide technical assistance to computer system users. Answer questions or resolve computer problems for clients in person, via telephone or remote location. May provide assistance concerning the use of computer hardware and software, including printing, installation, word processing, electronic mail and operating systems.

Computer Systems Analysts: Analyze science, engineering, business and all other data processing problems for application to electronic data processing systems. Analyze user requirements, procedures and problems to automate or improve existing systems and review computer system capabilities, work-flow and scheduling limitations. May analyze or recommend commercially available software. May supervise computer programmers.

Information Technology Manager

Information technology managers make sure computer departments run smoothly and efficiently. They may work with systems analysts to improve computer systems. They also manage databases, organise staff training, manage budgets, arrange computer maintenance and put into place backup systems in case an IT fault develops.

Work Activities: Information technology (IT) managers make sure that computer departments run smoothly and efficiently. They have overall responsibility for the use of IT within the company.

The IT manager first has to make sure that the company has all the right equipment it needs to be as efficient as possible. IT managers therefore need a very broad knowledge of different IT systems; they must keep up-to-date with advances in the technology. They are also likely to be in charge of a budget, spending money wisely to bring the most appropriate technology into the company. They work closely with equipment suppliers, negotiating the sale and any aftersales services, like technical support in case there are any faults with the equipment.

As well as buying new systems, IT managers keep a close watch on the technology the company already has. They think about the company's needs and identify areas where new technology could support people's work. They may ask a systems analyst to visit the company to do an in-depth study of the existing technology and come up with suggestions to improve the situation.

Information technology managers work as closely with people as they do with machines. They make sure people are properly trained and supported in their use of IT; they may ask a computer trainer to visit the company to teach people how to use a specific system or software product.

Managers are responsible for setting quality standards and for making sure people complete their work within deadlines and budget limitations.

They are also responsible for the accuracy and security of data within the organisation. A strict data protection law controls the use and security of information held on databases; it's up to the manager to make sure only authorised people can look at the data. Also, members of the public have the right to access any information about them on a company's database, so managers may have to negotiate this access with them.

IT managers must be able to cope quickly and efficiently if there are any problems with the company's computer systems. They must set up backup systems to make sure no data is lost if there is a fault.

Personal Qualities and Skills: To be an information technology manager, you must have a broad knowledge of computer systems and software products. Just as importantly, you must be willing to keep up-to-date with developments in IT.

You will need strong communication skills, to negotiate with equipment suppliers and to work closely with people throughout the organisation. You must be able to explain things clearly and concisely to people who may have little knowledge of computers and be able to ask the right questions to assess their training needs.

Information technology managers need very good organisation skills to plan work, arrange meetings with other professionals (like systems analysts or computer trainers) and set deadlines and targets.

You must be able to cope well under pressure, for example, if the system develops a fault.

Pay and Opportunities: The pay rates given below are approximate. IT Managers earn in the range of £24,500—£30,500 a year, rising to £41,000—£55,500. Higher earners can make around £73,500 a year. Salaries may include performance related pay, profit sharing or company bonuses.

IT managers usually work 35—37 hours Monday to Friday, though occasional late finishes may be required.

Jobs exist throughout the UK, with employers in industry and commerce, including banks, building societies and insurance companies and in the public sector with local and central government departments, the NHS and public utilities. Consultancy and fixed-term contract work can be available for experienced managers.

The following information is sourced from government statistics. The government's definition of types of job is slightly different to that used in this programme. For this type of job, the most relevant Government-defined occupation is 'Information and communication technology managers'.

In 2001 there were 9,400 people working as Information and communication technology managers in Scotland. 43 in every 10,000 employees working in Scotland were employed as Information and communication technology managers.

Estimates of projected future job openings requiring new entrants to the jobs market are available, but not at the level of detail of 'Information and communication technology managers'. It is estimated that over the five years between 2003 and 2008 there will be a need for 21,000 new employees to fill vacancies in the broader occupational type of 'Functional Managers'.

1 out of every 20 employees works part time in this type of job.

Entry Routes and Training: Most information technology managers are graduates, although few enter this job straight after graduation. Most people first gain experience in other IT careers, especially systems analysis (because this job involves working closely with people and using management skills).

Many managers are members of the Institute for the Management of Information Systems (IMIS). IMIS offers training leading to diploma, higher diploma and graduate diploma qualifications.

For entry to the graduate diploma, you should have the IMIS higher diploma, a Higher National Diploma or Higher National Certificate in Computing (though you will need to support the HND or HNC with two years' relevant work experience), or a degree in any subject plus at least one years' relevant experience. The graduate diploma covers Human and Computer Interaction, Database Design, Information Systems Engineering and Business, Systems and Strategy.

Qualifications: For entry to a degree course the minimum requirement is 3 Highers (A-C) plus Standard Grades (1-3) in 2 other subjects.

Entry requirements vary between courses and alternative qualifications may be accepted—check prospectuses for details.

Information technology managers have usually worked for some time in the computing industry, for example in systems analysis.

According to government statistics, people working in this job have the following qualifications. Higher Education: 6 out of 10 employees have their highest level of qualifications attained at degree level or equivalent or higher. Post-16 or Further Education: 2 out of 10 employees have their highest qualification at a level below a degree or higher degree or equivalent, but gained after the age of 16. School leaving age (16) qualifications or qualifications at SVQ3: 3 out of 10 employees gained their highest qualification at the age of 16 or have gained another qualification lower than a VQ level 3 since they were 16.

Adult Opportunities: There is no formal upper age limit for entry into this occupation.

Some employers will consider applicants with substantial relevant experience, even if they lack the usual academic or professional qualifications for entry.

Relevant experience can be as a systems designer/ programmer, engineer or analyst, with a focus on one or more specialised areas of IT, such as networks or databases.

Experience as a team leader can be an advantage for entry into management level posts.

For senior posts, taking the MBA (Master of Business Administration) can be an advantage, usually after a minimum of two years' IT management experience.

A range of manufacturer-accredited courses are available on an intensive basis, often flexible and part-time, including evenings and weekends.

Distance learning is also offered by Abacus Learning Systems, with courses in IT management training, plus the British Computer Society Professional Examination Certificate, Diploma and Graduate Diploma.

Suitable applicants aged 21 or over may do a college or university Access course. No formal qualifications are required to enter an Access course, but you should check individual course details. They lead to relevant degree/HND courses.

Education, Training and Degrees

Individuals looking for employment as information technology specialists generally must have at least a bachelor's degree in computer science, computer engineering, or a similar field. Certification in a specific technology is also helpful. Many companies, such as Microsoft, MySQL, Oracle, Cisco and Red Hat offer training and exams to help aspiring IT candidates become certified in their particular tools and technologies.

Individuals seeking a career in IT management should consider obtaining a master's degree in information systems or information technology, or an MBA with a focus on technology.

Explore Career Opportunities

The ongoing demand for online products and services, plus the emergence of new technologies, means that career opportunities in the field of information technology will continue to grow in the foreseeable future. Areas of particular interest and growth include IT security, the Linux market, open source technologies, wireless and mobile devices, wireless networking and telephony.

A number of career opportunities exist for those interested in the field of information technology. From entry-level jobs in technical support or the help desk, to mid-level jobs such as network administrator, computer programmer and Web developer, to the higher-level jobs such as database architect or information security specialist, numerous positions exist within the IT domain. Below are a few of the most popular professions in this field.

Information Technology Specialist

Information technology specialists set up computer systems and networks, test new solutions, troubleshoot problems that users may have, purchase new hardware and software and install and maintain security systems, among other responsibilities. They work with many people throughout a company, moving from computer to computer to find solutions to various computer problems.

Information Technology Manager

Information technology managers put both their technical and managerial skills to use by planning information strategies for a company, determining and working with budgets, coordinating projects and managing others.

Train for a new career in under two years!

LCCC offers many certificate training programmes that help you learn new career skills in a hurry. The short-term training opportunities are perfect for those who want to train for a good job, but aren't able to commit to long-term education or training.

Credits earned for many Certificate of Proficiency or Certificate of Completion programmes can be applied to a related LCCC associate's degree or an LCCC University Partnership bachelor's degree.

Information Technology Training & Certifications

You can earn certificates, diplomas, bachelor's degrees, master's degrees and doctoral degrees in almost all of the programmes within the information technology field. Programmes in which you may obtain certifications or degrees include computer security, network administration, computer support, systems developing and analyzing, computer programming, telecommunications, computer science and web design. Individuals with advanced information technology training and certifications should enjoy highly favourable employment prospects. Employers tend to seek information technology specialists who can combine strong technical skills with good interpersonal and business skills. In some instances, if you have the right experience along with information technology training and certification, you can work in many of the computer occupations regardless of your level of formal education.

Job Outlook: The information technology field will be one of the fastest growing occupations over the next few years. The demand for specialists will increase due to technology enhancements and the integration of new technologies. Businesses and other organizations will need workers with information technology training to not only implement more sophisticated and complex technology into their offices, but also to maintain the networks and teach others how to operate them.

IT and Certification Programmes

Information Technology Training: Search this directory for information about Information Technology Training and find the perfect campus or online degree programme. Please request free information from as many schools as necessary to make the right decision for you—it is risk free and there is no obligation.

Information technology training prepares you for an exciting profession that involves hardware, software, services and supporting infrastructure to manage and deliver information. Information technology includes all computers, voice, video and data networks and the equipment and staff needed to operate them. It also includes all costs associated with operating and providing information technology, as well as developing, purchasing, licensing and maintaining software. Some examples of information technology commonly used includes telephone and radio equipment, software and support for office automation systems and the computers that run them, server hardware and software and computers and network systems used for educational purposes.

Master Certificate & Certificate Programmes

Our IT programmes are designed to help the individual gain the skills and industry certification that will put them in demand by employers. Key industry certifications include CompTIA A+, Network+ and Linux+ and Microsoft MCP, MCSA, MCSE and MCDST. Programmes vary in length and depth of training. Your Admissions Representative will help you select a programme that best matches your current skills and career goals.

Oracle Database Administration Master Certificate Programme: Prepare for a rewarding career in managing information-one of businesses most valuable assets. As an Oracle Database Administrator you'll play a critical role managing and administering databases, setting up and implementing backup and recovery strategies and establishing and maintaining appropriate security systems. In our Oracle Database Administration programme, you'll learn how to perform the major tasks needed to administer and support these database systems. Understand Windows NT networking architectures and structures, PL/SQL (the language of Oracle) database administrative tasks, strategies for backing up an Oracle database, crash recovery procedures, security measures and ways of improving database performance through hands-on exercises. The Oracle Database Administration Programme uses the authorized Oracle curriculum. This programme is a ***Passport*** Programme-ask your counsellor for details.

Enterprise Solution Developer Master Certificate Programme: The Enterprise Solution Developer programme is targeted at the IT professional who wishes to upgrade their skills as a software developer to a true solution developer. Students will explore the Microsoft .Net framework with concentration on C# as well as the J2EE environment. This intense programme educates the student on the architectural approaches used in enterprise projects and the technical skills needed to build, support and integrate enterprise applications.

The programme focuses on technologies such as C#, JAVA, ASP.NET, ADO.NET, SQL Server, Oracle, XML and Web Services. Students who complete the programme have a sound, practical and hands-on experience as Enterprise Developers ready to fit into and succeed in today's complex information systems environment.

PC & Networking Support (CompTIA A+, Network+, Linux+ and Microsoft MCP Certifications) Master Certificate Programme: Get the skills needed to install and configure PC hardware such as disks, memory and network adapters and operating systems such as Windows and DOS. Learn how to install Microsoft Office, set up printing and troubleshoot common problems relating to Microsoft Office and e-mail. You'll also understand the fundamentals of computer networking, including LANs and WANs, TCP/IP and network administration. With this programme, you'll prepare for examinations, which lead to the CompTIA A+, Network+ and Linux+ Certifications, industry-wide vendor neutral, developed and sponsored by the Computing Technology Industry Association (CompTIA), as well as the entry-level Microsoft Certified Professional (MCP) certification.

PC & Networking Administration (CompTIA A+, Network+, Linux+ and Microsoft MCP, MCSA Certifications) Master Certificate Programme: Building on the PC & Networking Support classes, receive the career skills necessary to implement and administer Microsoft Windows 2003 Networking and Operating Systems Infrastructure. After successfully completing this programme you may pursue your Microsoft Certified System Administrator (MCSA) Certification.

PC & Networking Design (CompTIA A+, Network+, Linux+ and Microsoft MCP, MCSA, MCSE, MCDST Certifications) Master Certificate Programme: Building on the PC & Networking Administration classes, this programme trains you with the skills necessary to design and deploy Microsoft Windows 2003 Networking and Operating systems. After successfully completing this programme, you may pursue the most advanced certification from Microsoft—The Microsoft Certified System Engineer (MCSE) certification.

PC & Networking Design w/ Security (CompTIA A+, Network+, Linux+, Security +, MCP, MCSA, MCSE Certifications) Master Certificate Programme: A recent U.S. News & World Report article stated that Network Security is a "Profession in which jobs are projected to be plentiful for years to come." As one of the nation's top 8 career tracks, Network Security is a career with a future. Get the skills necessary to work in Network Security with this programme. You'll learn to design and analyze Network Security systems. After successful completion of this programme, you may pursue the Security Certified Network Professional (Security+) certification. This programme is a ***Passport*** Programme -ask your counsellor for details.

Careers, Jobs and Employment

Information Technology (IT) is a broad term that includes all aspects of managing and processing information and related technologies. Specifically, information technology professionals are responsible for designing, developing, supporting and managing computer hardware, computer software and information networks, such as the Internet. The realworld applications of information technologies can be found everywhere. In fact, IT is likely already a part of your life in ways you may not even be aware. Examples include computer software used to manage basic computer applications, computer generated animation in popular movies, networks and programmes that allow you to purchase online and satellites and systems that enable NASA to preform remote space exploration. There are a wide variety of career opportunities available for capable and experience IT professionals. Select a category below to review detailed job descriptions, career reviews, to identify useful technology degrees and to see employment forecasts.

How Outsourcing Affects Your Career in IT

In the United States, corporations plan to **outsource** many thousands of **Information Technology (IT)** jobs to outside firms. Most of these jobs will belong to so-called **offshore** organizations in India or Southeast Asia. The media buzz around

IT offshoring and outsourcing continues to grow and take on a colder, more fatalistic tone as time passes.

As a current Information Technology professional in the U.S., or a student considering a future career in IT, outsourcing is a business trend you must fully understand. Don't expect the trend to reverse any time in the forseeable future, but don't feel powerless to cope with the changes either.

Changes Coming with Information Technology Outsourcing

Five or ten years ago, workers were attracted to the Information Technology field given the

1. challenging and rewarding work
2. good pay
3. numerous opportunities, the promise of future growth and long term job stability

Outsourcing will alter and is already altering each of these IT career fundamentals:

1. The nature of the work will change dramatically with offshoring; the future may be equally rewarding, or it may prove wholly undesirable depending on one's individual interests and goals.
2. Information Technology salaries will increase in the countries that receive outsourcing contracts and will decrease in the U.S.
3. Likewise, the total number of IT jobs will increase in some countries and decrease in the U.S, most future growth will happen outside the U.S and job stability will remain unclear everywhere until the outsourcing business models mature.

How to Cope with Information Technology Outsourcing?

IT workers in the U.S. may already be witnessing some impacts of IT outsourcing, but the future impacts are likely to be much greater. What can you do to prepare? Consider the following ideas.

- *Don't Panic:* The prospect of job searches or career changes can be quite stressful to Information Technology workers.

IT students may understandably begin to question their choice of career. However, the more stress and worry a person takes on, paradoxically the more difficult it becomes to successfully reach their career goals.

- *Don't Wait for The Upturn:* So-called "experts" have been predicting a sharp upturn in the U.S. economy for several years. It's more likely that the sought-after economic recovery has already happened and we should expect to operate in the current climate for the foreseeable future.
- *Become a Generalist:* Years ago in Information Technology, specialization was king. Those with the heaviest technical backgrounds and loftiest job titles, like Enterprise Architects, commanded the highest salaries. Nowadays, a person is much better positioned if they are skilled in multiple areas of both technology and the business side of IT. Flexibility is now king.
- *Look to Smaller Organizations:* Fortune 500 companies will embark on the vast majority of outsourcing and offshoring deals. Outsourcing creates a substantial amount of overhead before the gains kick in and small companies can't afford to pay that price for the foreseeable future.
- *Start Your Own Business:* Uncertain economic times and times of big industry change are often the best ones for starting a new business, due to lower prices for capital, less competition and the natural emergence of big new market opportunities. All it takes is an entrepenurial attitude and a few good ideas.

Above all, whatever your chosen career path, strive to find happiness in your work. Don't fear the ongoing change in Information Technology just because others are afraid. Control your own destiny.

Starting or Building a Career in Computer Networking

Many view computer networking as one of the best and "hottest" career fields available today. Some claim that a serious shortage of qualified people to fill these networking jobs exists and these claims may lure some people into the fray hoping for an easy position with a fast-growing company.

Don't be fooled! Debates over the actual extent of any "shortages" aside, networking involves mostly hard work and competition for the high-quality positions will always be strong. Continue reading to learn more about beginning or expanding a career in networking and pick up some valuable job-hunting tips that also apply to many other types of technical careers.

Job Titles: Several types of positions exist in networking, each with different average salaries and long-term potential and one should possess a clear understanding of these. Unfortunately, job titles in networking and in Information Technology (IT) generally, often lead to confusion among beginners and experienced folks alike.

Bland, vague or overly bombastic titles often fail to describe the actual work assignments of a person in this field.

The basic job titles one sees for computer networking and networking-related positions include

- Network Administrator
- Network (Systems) Engineer
- Network (Service) Technician
- Network Programmer/Analyst
- Network/Information Systems Manager

The Network Administrator: In general, network administrators configure and manage LANs and sometimes WANs. The job descriptions for administrators can be detailed and sometimes downright intimidating! Consider the following description that, although fictitious, represents a fairly typical posting:

Network Administrator—Hobo Computing

"Candidate will be responsible for analysis, installation and configuration of company networks. Daily activities include monitoring network performance, troubleshooting problems and maintaining network security.

Other activities include assisting customers with operating systems and network adapters, configuring routers, switches and firewalls and evaluating third-party tools."

Needless to say, a person early in their career often lacks experience in a majority of these categories. Most employers do not expect candidates to possess in-depth knowledge of all areas listed in the job posting, though, so a person should remain undeterred by the long, sweeping job descriptions they will inevitably encounter.

Comparing Roles and Responsibilities: The job function of a Network Engineer differs little from that of a Network Administrator. Company A may use one title while Company B uses the other to refer to essentially the same position. Some companies even use the two titles interchangeably. Firms making a distinction between the two often stipulate that administrators focus on the day-to-day management of networks, whereas network engineers focus primarily on system upgrades, evaluating vendor products, security testing and so on.

A Network Technician tends to focus more on the setup, troubleshooting and repair of specific hardware and software products. Service Technicians in particular often must travel to remote customer sites to perform "field" upgrades and support. Again, though, some firms blur the line between technicians and engineers or administrators.

Network Programmer/Analysts generally write software programmes or scripts that aid in network analysis, such as diagnostics or monitoring utilities. They also specialize in evaluating third-party products and integrating new software technologies into an existing network environment or to build a new environment.

Managers supervise the work of adminstrators, engineers, technicians and/or programmers. Network/Information Systems Managers also focus on longer-range planning and strategy considerations.

Salaries for networking positions depend on many factors such as the hiring organization, local market conditions, a person's experience and skill level and so on.

High School and College Education: Those interested in networking careers can benefit greatly from earning a college degree. Most university programmes don't offer a degree in Computer Networking *per se* and the precise name of the degree varies significantly from institution to institution. Four-year degree programmes suitable for the computer networking field usually involve a variation on one of the following:

- Computer Science
- Electrical and Computer Engineering
- Information Systems
- Communications Science
- Telecommunications, Telecommunications Management
- Telecomputing

As an alternative to a general four-year degree (that covers a variety of technical subjects besides computer networking), some institutions offer shorter-term programmes focused specifically on networking topics.

Until recently, computer networking courses were only found in post-secondary education. Nowadays, though, high school students have the opportunity to take networking courses too. These classes can be quite substantial, involving among other things configuring routers and switches, installing wire, network diagnostics, monitoring network activity and working with various network protocols and operating systems.

Which Programme Is Best?: Is a college degree worth the investment, or is a shorter, more focused curriculum the way to go? Opinions vary. A four-degree can demonstrate to prospective employers a level of dedication and long-term flexibility that a short programme cannot. On the other hand, a more focused programme can teach the basic networking skills quickly and allow more time for on-the-job experience.

Certifications: Network administrators and managers in particular have grown fond of networking-based certifications like Microsoft MCSE and Cisco CCNA. In general, to gain and keep a certification one must pass a lengthy (usually multiple-choice question) paper exam, then pass recertification exams at periodic intervals (usually every two or three years). A person has the choice of preparing for the exam through self-study or by enrolling in a certification course or "programme" run by a training organization (sometimes within high-tech companies themselves). Taking any certification exam involves paying a test "sitting" fee (usually in the range of $100 to $300 USD) and employers sometimes reimburse their employees for this cost.

Certifications are designed to accredit someone for a certain amount of industry experience that they've already gained. Some of the programmes will even make recommendations to this effect, typically one to two years of prior background for the entry-level certifications. However, experience is not strictly required. Some have criticized the entry-level exams for being too "bookish" in this respect, too easy to pass without prior hands-on experience.

Which certification is best? MCSE? CCNA? Something else? Again, the answer depends on the individual's interests and also the preferences of hiring companies. Some ambitious students of networking avoid this problem by acquiring multiple certifications... sometimes as many as five or more! Be aware, though, that certifications are an incomplete substitute for formal education and industry experience. Ideally, one will acquire a few certifications as part of a balanced overall mix of education and career experience.

Many companies, particularly larger ones, offer their employees ongoing training opportunities. The employer will either build their own courses or will bring in an outside company to hold the training. These courses are typically focused on a specific product technology or tool, or on the specific technical information needed to pass a certification exam. One could argue it is preferable for the beginning networker to focus on general technologies at first rather than certifications, as companies in these case likely prefer to train employees "their own way" anyhow.

Networking Experience: The common lament of job seekers, that "employers only hire people with experience, yet the only way to gain experience is to get hired" applies in the computer networking field as well. Despite optimistic statements that one hears frequently regarding the number of available jobs in IT, landing an entry-level position can still prove difficult and frustrating.

One way to gain networking experience is to pursue a full-time programming or help desk "internship" during the summer months, or a part-time "work study" job at school. An internship may not pay well initially, the work may turn out to be relatively uninteresting and it is very likely one will not be able to finish any substantial project during the limited time there. However, the most important factor to consider is the training and hands-on experience such a job offers. The mere fact a person invests their time in this way, demonstrates the dedication and interest employers like to see.

The better the position, the more likely multiple candidates will apply for it, even if the job entails only part-time work. A good way to "stand out" from the competition is to demonstrate prior work and accomplishments, even if these involve projects done on one's own time. A person can start with a class project, for example and extend it in some way. Or they can create their own personal projects, experimenting with networking administration tools and scripts, for example.

Explaining Experience: One of the most overlooked skills in computer networking is the ability to explain technical information. Whether verbally, through e-mail, or in formal writing, networkers that communicate well gain a significant advantage in building their careers.

For the beginning networker, the most obvious benefit of good communications skills is realized in job interviews. Being able to talk with people about technical subjects can be hard to do, but as one gains skill in answering impromptu questions, one builds confidence and relaxes, making one that much better prepared for career advancement. It is a good idea to periodically engage in job interviews for this reason, even if the position involved does not seem particularly appealing. Likewise one should also consider visiting local job fairs occasionally.

Technologies: One of the most common questions asked by beginning networkers is "Which technology should I focus on first? Microsoft? UNIX? Cisco? Novell?" As with certifications, preferences vary from company to company and person to person.

One way for a person to answer this question is to start with the technology that appears most interesting to them personally. Researching a company that one plans to interview with and choosing a technology that the company deems important, is another way. Ultimately it probably matters little which networking technology one learns first. More importantly, one should acknowledge that technology changes rapidly and that the person who can enjoy a successful career by learning about only one technology is rare indeed.

Focus on the Basics: Computer networking involves a certain number of fundamental technologies. These technologies form the basis of many networking courses. Regardless of the form of education one chooses to invest in, one's career will always benefit from deeper study of technologies like IP and TCP/IP, the OSI model, Ethernet, internet working and others listed on this site, whether through formal coursework or through self-study.

Conclusion: Some people have asserted that networking (and IT generally) is a "young person's game," and that companies generally prefer to turn over their employee base periodically, to bring in younger, more affordable workers. This concept might sound appealing to some, but if it were true, it would make networking careers less inviting to most people.

Realistically, the field of computer networking presents so much complexity and involves such a wide range of technologies, that most serious companies should value both experienced employees and ambitious new employees highly. In fact, an effective career strategy involves seeking out more experienced people in one's field and learning new skills from these *mentors*.

Many firms view four-years degrees as a sign of commitment to the field. Network technology changes very fast, so employers care both about a person's current knowledge and also their ability to learn and adapt for the future. Certifications effectively prove current knowledge, but college degrees best demonstrate one's general learning ability.

Self-study in networking is always effective and underrated by many. By making contacts with those in networking careers, either people in one's local area, or individuals or sites on the Internet, one can quickly acquire a wealth of information ranging from technical details, to advice on writing a resume, to advice on specific hiring companies, schools and so on.

Management Information Systems (MIS)

With offices in 85 countries and with more than 1,500 employees, our systems need to be fast, effective and comprehensive. Alltech is all about communication.

Information Technology has been a key enabler in facilitating the rapid growth of the company. One of our key functions is the development of effective information systems to satisfy our internal and external demands. Dealing with the challenges of the information age requires a dynamic team of individuals working in concert around the world.

Carlos joined Alltech as MIS Manager for Latin America in 2000. Based in Kentucky, he manages eleven different countries, driving all of them through a period of growth. Carlos ensures that each of them possess the same high-level technological infrastructure required to support the continued international growth of Alltech. During the last three years he has been afforded the opportunity to redesign the networks and update the equipment within all of the countries for which he is responsible. Two of these countries, Brazil and Mexico, represent some of Alltech's biggest sales markets and through Alltech MIS, Carlos works with and manages some excellent IT professionals. In each of the other nine countries, he manages relationships with local companies that provide Alltech with front-line IT support.

Industry Organizations

World Information Technology and Services Alliance (WITSA) is a consortium of over 60 information technology (IT) industry associations from economies around the world. Founded in 1978 and originally known as the World Computing Services Industry Association, WITSA has increasingly assumed an active advocacy role in international public policy issues affecting the creation of a robust global information infrastructure.

The Information Technology Association of America (ITAA) is an industry trade group for several U.S. information technology companies.

Founded in 1961 as the Association of Data Processing Services Organizations (ADAPSO), the Information Technology Association of America (ITAA) provides global public policy, business networking and national leadership to promote the continued rapid growth of the IT industry. ITAA consists of approximately 325 corporate members throughout the U.S. and is secretariat of the World Information Technology and Services Alliance (WITSA), a global network of 67 countries' IT associations.

NASSCOM is the Industry body/chamber of commerce for Information Technology Companies in India. It has been instrumental in helping the Indian Information Technology Industry grow.

Career Profile: Application Architect

Application Architects design, construct, deploy and maintain applications that target a specific business need. Those in this career design and implement business object models and application services, determine the requirements for these services and identify the techniques and technologies that need to be applied to help define a system and its operational requirements. They must be able to identify the types, organization and interactions of the software components that will be responsible for delivering the defined user services.

Information Technology: HSBC in Hong Kong has been pursuing an aggressive business strategy, particularly in Personal Financial Services, Commercial Banking and Wealth Management HSBC in Hong Kong has been pursuing an aggressive business strategy, particularly in Personal Financial Services, Commercial Banking and Wealth Management. As IT is a key enabler of this strategy, the demand for IT development resources to support its development and implementation has increased significantly.

HTSA (HSBC Technology Services Asia-Pacific) is made up of over 30 major departments, with about 2,800 staff. These departments increase the operational efficiency of HSBC in the Asia-Pacific region and improve and increase the range of services offered to customers through the design, development, installation, operation and maintenance of appropriate computer systems. Each department is responsible for a distinct area of systems development or support. The departments are grouped by types of equipment/applications and by end-users served.

IT Development: IT Development is responsible for the design and development of Banking Systems and Group Systems for Personal Financial Services and Commercial Banking and also looks after the deployment of Enterprise Data. To ensure that the systems meet the unique requirements of our business, it is our best practice to deploy Group Systems or develop our major software applications and systems internally rather than buying third-party packages.

To ensure that our applications are efficiently and professionally constructed, we have invested heavily in the use of modern software tools. At the same time, we encourage a full understanding of the technical environment. Where efficiency is paramount, assembly languages and other low level tools are employed.

Programming languages we use include COBOL, PL/1, RPG, SQL, C, C++, JAVA, Visual Basic and Assembler and control languages JCL, CL, DCL and REXX. Systems we adopt include z/OS, OS/390, TSO, CICS, OS/400, OS/2, Windows, UNIX and CWD. We also employ DB2, IDMS, DB/400, SQL Server, Sybase and ORACLE.

IT Operations: IT Operations comprise Computer Operations, Infrastructure and Telecommunications teams. Our mainframe computers are IBM and IBM-compatibles. We use IBM iSeries mid-range and mini-computers. We use IBM RS/6000, HP, Domino and MS Windows NT servers. Our Microcomputers and Terminals are IBM PC/Compatibles/LAN, OS/2 Banking Terminals, NCR ATMs, Unix/Windows NT Workstations and NCR Cash Deposit Machine. In our network, the major components are Nortel Passport/Cisco Routers. Our Group Router Network (GRN) covers the major/larger offices, whilst Global Data Network (GDN) covers the branch networks globally and comprises over 10,000 Cisco routers, in 76 countries and territories.

IT General: Other IT functional areas include IT Architecture, Information Security, IT Quality, Finance and Planning. These areas serve the important functions of aligning business strategies with emerging technologies, facilitating the implementation of Group IT security standards, improving transparency of IT charges and aligning quality management practices across Asia-Pacific regions and Group standards.

Corporate, Investment Banking and Markets (CIBM) IT HK

Global CIBM IT provides software solutions to our Corporate, Investment Banking and Markets business globally. This is a complex and fast-paced business, involving high-value transactions that contribute to one-third of the Bank's total profits. CIBM IT HK is responsible for supporting the CIBM business in Hong Kong and overseeing IT activities for CIBM businesses in over 30 entities across more than 20 Asia-Pacific countries and territories, as well as working closely with our other regional CIBM IT centres in London, France and New York. CIBM IT prides itself on the early adoption of advanced new technologies, fostering an environment of continuous development.

Those who excel within CIBM IT in HSBC should be willing to face challenges in a demanding, high-pressure role and possess strong problem solving abilities, a highly analytical mindset and an enthusiasm for keeping abreast of emerging technologies. Far from a stereotypical and sedentary programming function, our people often travel globally and coordinate with our product teams in Asia Pacific and other regions worldwide.

IT Graduate Opportunities

Training and Development: People are our most valuable resources. The enormous range of knowledge and expertise our staff possess is absolutely vital to the very existence and future of our organisation. IT therefore ensures that this knowledge and expertise are carefully nurtured and the personal needs of our people are recognised and met.

With our emphasis on teamwork and on ensuring that we meet our user needs, we look for people who are good team players and are able to communicate effectively with both technical and non-technical people. Graduates majoring in IT- and computer-related studies who have strong analytical skills and good attention to detail must, above all, have a strong commitment to a career at the leading edge of the IT profession. For these people, our policy to fill senior positions by promotion from within means that the opportunities for career advancement are excellent.

Training plays a key role. Initial training consists of a one-month induction programme, comprising full-time classroom lectures delivered by experienced staff, various video courses and course projects to practise teamwork and to familiarise staff with the development environment. Staff can continue learning with classroom training, self-study training and on-the-job training. IT PATH courses in Information Processing, Banking Applications, Technical Skills and Human Resources Development are available to help employees as their careers progress.

Programmers with a higher diploma can progress to Systems Analyst/Programmer positions after 12 months. After 24 months' initial training, Systems Analysts and Programmers who hold a degree become eligible for promotion to IT Officer. As IT Officers progress and develop, they take increasing responsibility for analysis, design and project/team leadership on more complex systems, up to and possibly beyond department management.

Benefits and Applications: HSBC offers job security, prospective career development, a pleasant working environment and attractive fringe benefits. Among our benefits are: Housing Loan Scheme, Medical Insurance, Variable Incentives/Bonus-related Share Options Scheme, Savings-related Share Options Scheme, Local Staff Defined Contribution Retirement Scheme/MPF, 22 days' Annual Leave and Credit Facilities (including overdrafts and credit cards).

To Apply: Graduates with little or no working experience who are interested in entry-level positions, please download and complete the application form as a PDF file or Word document.

IT Development: IT Development is responsible for the design and development of Banking Systems and Group Systems for Personal Financial Services and Commercial Banking and also looks after the deployment of Enterprise Data. To ensure that the systems meet the unique requirements of our business, it is our best practice to deploy Group Systems or develop our major software applications and systems internally rather than buying third-party packages.

To ensure that our applications are efficiently and professionally constructed, we have invested heavily in the use of modern software tools. At the same time, we encourage a full understanding of the technical environment. Where efficiency is paramount, assembly languages and other low level tools are employed.

Programming languages we use include COBOL, PL/1, RPG, SQL, C, C++, JAVA, Visual Basic and Assembler and control languages JCL, CL, DCL and REXX. Systems we adopt include z/OS, OS/390, TSO, CICS, OS/400, OS/2, Windows, UNIX and CWD. We also employ DB2, IDMS, DB/400, SQL Server, Sybase and ORACLE.

IT Operations: IT Operations comprise Computer Operations, Infrastructure and Telecommunications teams. Our mainframe computers are IBM and IBM-compatibles. We use IBM iSeries mid-range and mini-computers. We use IBM RS/6000, HP, Domino and MS Windows NT servers. Our Microcomputers and Terminals are IBM PC/Compatibles/LAN, OS/2 Banking Terminals, NCR ATMs, Unix/Windows NT Workstations and NCR Cash Deposit Machine. In our network, the major components are Nortel Passport/Cisco Routers. Our Group Router Network (GRN) covers the major/larger offices, whilst Global Data Network (GDN) covers the branch networks globally and comprises over 10,000 Cisco routers, in 76 countries and territories.

IT General: Other IT functional areas include IT Architecture, Information Security, IT Quality, Finance and Planning.

These areas serve the important functions of aligning business strategies with emerging technologies, facilitating the implementation of Group IT security standards, improving transparency of IT charges and aligning quality management practices across Asia-Pacific regions and Group standards.

Training and Professional Qualifications

On-the-job training and in-house courses are typically provided to help you develop technical and business skills, though external courses may be necessary to familiarise you with specific programming languages and business software. Depending on your role, you may also be offered training in project management, or in softer skills such as communication, team leading and presentations.

The British Computer Society (BCS) offers professional qualifications. e-skills UK—The Sector Skills Council for IT and Telecoms has also launched the Graduate Professional Development Award (GPDA), which combines National Vocational Qualification (NVQ) and key skill units to complement honours degrees.

Rewards: Salaries for IT professionals typically start in the region of £19,000—£25,000, progressing to £30,000—£45,000 for those at senior level with experience (for example, after 10-15 years). Salaries for senior analysts and programmers may be higher in this, the financial sector and in London, the South East and the Midlands, where they could top £80,000.

Individuals with good business skills who move into more strategic business development roles are also likely to command higher salaries.

Prospects: Career progression for most in IT roles is mainly into management via team leadership and project management. You may choose to remain in one area of technical specialisation or to broaden your career options into other IT, business development, customer-related or management functions.

Computer Programmers

Significant Points: Sixty-seven percent of computer programmers held a college or higher degree in 2004; nearly half held a bachelor's degree and about 1 in 5 held a graduate degree.

Employment is expected to grow much more slowly than that for other computer specialists.

Prospects likely will be best for college graduates with knowledge of a variety of programming languages and tools; those with less formal education or its equivalent in work experience are apt to face strong competition for programming jobs.

Nature of the Work: Computer programmers write, test and maintain the detailed instructions, called programmes, that computers must follow to perform their functions. Programmers also conceive, design and test logical structures for solving problems by computer. Many technical innovations in programming—advanced computing technologies and sophisticated new languages and programming tools—have redefined the role of a programmer and elevated much of the programming work done today. Job titles and descriptions may vary, depending on the organization. In this occupational statement, *computer programmers* are individuals whose main job function is programming; this group has a wide range of responsibilities and educational backgrounds.

Computer programmes tell the computer what to do—which information to identify and access, how to process it and what equipment to use. Programmes vary widely depending on the type of information to be accessed or generated. For example, the instructions involved in updating financial records are very different from those required to duplicate conditions on an aircraft for pilots training in a flight simulator. Although simple programmes can be written in a few hours, programmes that use complex mathematical formulas whose solutions can only be approximated or that draw data from many existing systems may require more than a year of work. In most cases, several programmers work together as a team under a senior programmer's supervision.

Programmers write programmes according to the specifications determined primarily by computer software engineers and systems analysts. After the design process is complete, it is the job of the programmer to convert that design into a logical series of instructions that the computer can follow.

The programmer codes these instructions in a conventional programming language such as COBOL; an artificial intelligence language such as Prolog; or one of the most advanced object-oriented languages, such as Java, C++, or ACTOR. Different programming languages are used depending on the purpose of the programme.

COBOL, for example, is commonly used for business applications, whereas Fortran (short for "formula translation") is used in science and engineering. C++ is widely used for both scientific and business applications. Extensible Markup Language (XML) has become a popular programming tool for Web programmers, along with J2EE (Java 2 Platform). Programmers generally know more than one programming language and, because many languages are similar, they often can learn new languages relatively easily.

In practice, programmers often are referred to by the language they know, such as Java programmers, or by the type of function they perform or environment in which they work—for example, database programmers, mainframe programmers, or Web programmers.

Many programmers update, repair, modify and expand existing programmes. When making changes to a section of code, called a routine, programmers need to make other users aware of the task that the routine is to perform. They do this by inserting comments in the coded instructions so that others can understand the programme. Many programmers use computer-assisted software engineering (CASE) tools to automate much of the coding process. These tools enable a programmer to concentrate on writing the unique parts of the programme, because the tools automate various pieces of the programme being built. CASE tools generate whole sections of code automatically, rather than line by line. Programmers also use libraries of basic code that can be modified or customized for a specific application. This approach yields more reliable and consistent programmes and increases programmers' productivity by eliminating some routine steps.

Programmers test a programme by running it to ensure that the instructions are correct and that the programme produces the desired outcome. If errors do occur, the programmer must make the appropriate change and re-check the programme until it produces the correct results.

This process is called testing and debugging. Programmers may continue to fix these problems throughout the life of a programme. Programmers working in a mainframe environment, which involves a large centralized computer, may prepare instructions for a computer operator who will run the programme. Programmers also may contribute to a manual for persons who will be using the programme.

Computer programmers often are grouped into two broad types—applications programmers and systems programmers. *Applications programmers* write programmes to handle a specific job, such as a programme to track inventory within an organization. They also may revise existing packaged software or customize generic applications which are frequently purchased from vendors.

Systems programmers, in contrast, write programmes to maintain and control computer systems software, such as operating systems, networked systems and database systems. These workers make changes in the instructions that determine how the network, workstations and central processing unit of the system handle the various jobs they have been given and how they communicate with peripheral equipment such as terminals, printers and disk drives.

Because of their knowledge of the entire computer system, systems programmers often help applications programmers determine the source of problems that may occur with their programmes.

Programmers in software development companies may work directly with experts from various fields to create software—

either programmes designed for specific clients or packaged software for general use—ranging from games and educational software to programmes for desktop publishing and financial planning. Programming of packaged software constitutes one of the most rapidly growing segments of the computer services industry.

In some organizations, particularly small ones, workers commonly known as *programmer-analysts* are responsible for both the systems analysis and the actual programming work. Advanced programming languages and new object-oriented programming capabilities are increasing the efficiency and productivity of both programmers and users. The transition from a mainframe environment to one that is based primarily on personal computers (PCs) has blurred the once rigid distinction between the programmer and the user. Increasingly, adept end users are taking over many of the tasks previously performed by programmers. For example, the growing use of packaged software, such as spreadsheet and database management software packages, allows users to write simple programmes to access data and perform calculations.

Working Conditions: Programmers generally work in offices in comfortable surroundings. Many programmers may work long hours or weekends to meet deadlines or fix critical problems that occur during off hours. Telecommuting is becoming common for a wide range of computer professionals, including computer programmers. As computer networks expand, more programmers are able to make corrections or fix problems remotely using modems, e-mail and the Internet to connect to a customer's computer.

Like other workers who spend long periods in front of a computer terminal typing at a keyboard, programmers are susceptible to eyestrain, back discomfort and hand and wrist problems such as carpal tunnel syndrome.

Training, Other Qualifications and Advancement: Although there are many training paths available for programmers, mainly because employers' needs are so varied, the level of education and experience employers seek has been rising due to the growing number of qualified applicants and the specialization involved with most programming tasks. Bachelor's degrees are commonly required, although some programmers may qualify for certain jobs with 2-year degrees or certificates. The associate degree is a widely used entry-level credential for prospective computer programmers. Most community colleges and many independent technical institutes and proprietary schools offer an associate degree in computer science or a related information technology field.

Employers primarily are interested in programming knowledge and computer programmers can become certified in a programming language such as C++ or Java. College graduates who are interested in changing careers or developing an area of expertise also may return to a 2-year community college or technical school for additional training. In the absence of a degree, substantial specialized experience or expertise may be needed. Even when hiring programmers with a degree, employers appear to place more emphasis on previous experience.

Some computer programmers hold a college degree in computer science, mathematics, or information systems, whereas others have taken special courses in computer programming to supplement their degree in a field such as accounting, inventory control, or another area of business. As the level of education and training required by employers continues to rise, the proportion of programmers with a college degree should increase in the future. As indicated by the following tabulation, more than two-thirds of computer programmers had a bachelor's or higher degree in 2004.

High school graduate or less	8.3%
Some college, no degree	14.1
Associate degree	10.2
Bachelor's degree	49.1
Graduate degree	18.3

Required skills vary from job to job, but the demand for various skills generally is driven by changes in technology. Employers using computers for scientific or engineering applications usually prefer college graduates who have degrees in computer or information science, mathematics, engineering, or the physical sciences. Graduate degrees in related fields are required for some jobs. Employers who use computers for business applications prefer to hire people who have had college courses in management information systems and business and who possess strong programming skills.

Although knowledge of traditional languages still is important, employers are placing increasing emphasis on newer, object-oriented programming languages and tools such as C++ and Java. Additionally, employers are seeking persons familiar with fourth-generation and fifth-generation languages that involve graphic user interface and systems programming. Employers also prefer applicants who have general business skills and experience related to the operations of the firm. Students can improve their employment prospects by participating in a college work-study programme or by undertaking an internship.

Most systems programmers hold a 4-year degree in computer science. Extensive knowledge of a variety of operating systems is essential for such workers. This includes being able to configure an operating system to work with different types of hardware and having the skills needed to adapt the operating system to best meet the needs of a particular organization. Systems programmers also must be able to work with database systems, such as DB2, Oracle, or Sybase.

When hiring programmers, employers look for people with the necessary programming skills who can think logically and pay close attention to detail. The job calls for patience, persistence and the ability to work on exacting analytical work, especially under pressure. Ingenuity and creativity are particularly important when programmers design solutions and test their work for potential failures. The ability to work with abstract concepts and to do technical analysis is especially important for systems programmers because they work with the software that controls the computer's operation. Because programmers are expected to work in teams and interact directly with users, employers want programmers who are able to communicate with nontechnical personnel.

Entry-level or junior programmers may work alone on simple assignments after some initial instruction, or they may be assigned to work on a team with more experienced programmers. Either way, beginning programmers generally must work under close supervision. Because technology changes so rapidly, programmers must continuously update their knowledge and skills by taking courses sponsored by their employer or by software vendors, or offered through local community colleges and universities.

For skilled workers who keep up to date with the latest technology, the prospects for advancement are good. In large organizations, programmers may be promoted to lead programmer and be given supervisory responsibilities. Some applications programmers may move into systems programming after they gain experience and take courses in systems software. With general business experience, programmers may become programmer-analysts or systems analysts or be promoted to managerial positions. Other programmers, with specialized knowledge and experience with a language or operating system, may work in research and development for multimedia or Internet technology and may even become computer software engineers. As employers increasingly contract with outside firms to do programming jobs, more opportunities should arise for experienced programmers with expertise in a specific area to work as consultants.

Certification is a way to demonstrate a level of competence and may provide a jobseeker with a competitive advantage. In addition to language-specific certificates that a programmer can obtain, product vendors or software firms also offer certification and may require professionals who work with their products to be certified. Voluntary certification also is available through various other organizations.

Employment: Computer programmers held about 455,000 jobs in 2004. Programmers are employed in almost every industry, but the largest concentration is in computer systems design and related services. Large numbers of programmers also work for telecommunications companies, software publishers, financial institutions, insurance carriers, educational institutions and government agencies. Many computer programmers are employed on a temporary or contract basis or work as independent consultants, providing companies expertise with new programming languages or specialized areas of application.

Rather than hiring programmers as permanent employees and then laying them off after a job is completed, employers can contract with temporary help agencies, with consulting firms, or with programmers themselves. A marketing firm, for example, may require programming services only to write and debug the software necessary to get a new customer database running. Bringing in an independent contractor or consultant with experience in a new or advanced programming language enables the firm to complete the job without having to retrain existing workers. Such jobs may last anywhere from several weeks to a year or longer. There were 25,000 self-employed computer programmers in 2004.

Job Outlook: As programming tasks become increasingly sophisticated and additional levels of skill and experience are demanded by employers, graduates of 2-year programmes and people with less than a 2-year degree or its equivalent in work experience will face strong competition for programming jobs. Competition for entry-level positions, however, also can affect applicants with a bachelor's degree.

Prospects should be best for college graduates with knowledge of and experience working with, a variety of programming languages and tools—including C++ and other object-oriented languages such as Java, as well as newer, domain-specific languages that apply to computer networking, database management and Internet application development. Obtaining vendor-specific or language-specific certification also can provide a competitive edge.

Because demand fluctuates with employers' needs, jobseekers should keep up to date with the latest skills and technologies. Individuals who want to become programmers can enhance their prospects by combining the appropriate formal training with practical work experience.

Employment of programmers is expected to grow more slowly than the average for all occupations through the year 2014. Sophisticated computer software now has the capability to write basic code, eliminating the need for many programmers to do this routine work. The consolidation and centralization of systems and applications, developments in packaged software, advances in programming languages and tools and the growing ability of users to design, write and implement more of their own programmes mean that more of the programming functions can be transferred from programmers to other types of information workers, such as computer software engineers.

Another factor limiting growth in employment is the outsourcing of these jobs to other countries. Computer programmers can perform their job function from anywhere in the world and can digitally transmit their programmes to any location via e-mail. Programmers are at a much higher risk of having their jobs outsourced abroad than are workers involved in more complex and sophisticated information technology functions, such as software engineering, because computer programming has become an international language, requiring little localized or specialized knowledge. Additionally, the work of computer programmers can be routinized, once knowledge of a particular programming language is mastered.

Nevertheless, employers will continue to need programmers who have strong technical skills and who understand an employer's business and its programming requirements. This means that programmers will have to keep abreast of changing programming languages and techniques. Given the importance of networking and the expansion of client/server, Web-based and wireless environments, organizations will look for programmers who can support data communications and help implement electronic commerce and intranet strategies.

Demand for programmers with strong object-oriented programming capabilities and technical specialization in areas such as client/server programming, wireless applications, multimedia technology and graphic user interface likely will stem from the expansion of intranets, extranets and Internet applications. Programmers also will be needed to create and maintain expert systems and embed these technologies in more products. Finally, a growing emphasis on cybersecurity will lead to increased demand for programmers who are familiar with digital security issues and skilled in using appropriate security technology.

Jobs for both systems and applications programmers should be most plentiful in data-processing service firms, software houses and computer consulting businesses. These types of establishments are part of computer systems design and related services and software publishers, which are projected to be among the fastest growing industries in the economy over the 2004-14 period.

As organizations attempt to control costs and keep up with changing technology, they will need programmers to assist in conversions to new computer languages and systems. In addition, numerous job openings will result from the need to replace programmers who leave the labour force or transfer to other occupations such as manager or systems analyst.

Earnings: Median annual earnings of computer programmers were $62,890 in May 2004. The middle 50 percent earned between $47,580 and $81,280 a year. The lowest 10 percent earned less than $36,470; the highest 10 percent earned more than $99,610. Median annual earnings in the industries employing the largest numbers of computer programmers in May 2004 are shown below:

Software publishers	$73,060
Computer systems design and related services	67,600
Data processing, hosting and related services	64,540
Insurance carriers	62,990
Management of companies and enterprises	62,160

According to the National Association of Colleges and Employers, starting salary offers for graduates with a bachelor's degree in computer science averaged $50,820 a year in 2005.

According to Robert Half International, a firm providing specialized staffing services, average annual starting salaries in 2005 ranged from $52,500 to $83,250 for applications development programmers/analysts and from $55,000 to $88,250 for software developers. Average starting salaries for mainframe systems programmers ranged from $50,250 to $67,500 in 2005.

Computer Software Engineers

Significant Points: Computer software engineers are projected to be one of the fastest growing occupations over the 2004-14 period.

Very good opportunities are expected for college graduates with at least a bachelor's degree in computer engineering or computer science and with practical work experience.

Computer software engineers must continually strive to acquire new skills in conjunction with the rapid changes that are occurring in computer technology.

Nature of the Work: The explosive impact of computers and information technology on our everyday lives has generated a need to design and develop new computer software systems and to incorporate new technologies into a rapidly growing range of applications. The tasks performed by workers known as computer software engineers evolve quickly, reflecting new areas of specialization or changes in technology, as well as the preferences and practices of employers.

Computer software engineers apply the principles and techniques of computer science, engineering and mathematical analysis to the design, development, testing and evaluation of the software and systems that enable computers to perform their many applications.

Software engineers working in applications or systems development analyze users' needs and design, construct, test and maintain computer applications software or systems. Software engineers can be involved in the design and development of many types of software, including software for operating systems and network distribution and compilers, which convert programmes for execution on a computer. In programming, or coding, software engineers instruct a computer, line by line, how to perform a function. They also solve technical problems that arise. Software engineers must possess strong programming skills, but are more concerned with developing algorithms and analyzing and solving programming problems than with actually writing code.

Computer applications software engineers analyze users' needs and design, construct and maintain general computer applications software or specialized utility programmes. These workers use different programming languages, depending on the purpose of the programme.

The programming languages most often used are C, C++ and Java, with Fortran and COBOL used less commonly. Some software engineers develop both packaged systems and systems software or create customized applications.

Computer systems software engineers coordinate the construction and maintenance of a company's computer systems and plan their future growth. Working with the company, they coordinate each department's computer needs—ordering, inventory, billing and payroll recordkeeping, for example—and make suggestions about its technical direction. They also might set up the company's intranets—networks that link computers within the organization and ease communication among the various departments.

Systems software engineers work for companies that configure, implement and install complete computer systems. These workers may be members of the marketing or sales staff, serving as the primary technical resource for sales workers and customers.

They also may be involved in product sales and in providing their customers with continuing technical support. Since the selling of complex computer systems often requires substantial customization for the purchaser's organization, software engineers help to explain the requirements necessary for installing and operating the new system in the purchaser's computing environment. In addition, systems software engineers are responsible for ensuring security across the systems they are configuring.

Computer software engineers often work as part of a team that designs new hardware, software and systems. A core team may comprise engineering, marketing, manufacturing and design people, who work together until the product is released.

Working Conditions: Computer software engineers normally work in well-lighted and comfortable offices or laboratories in which computer equipment is located. Most software engineers work at least 40 hours a week; however, due to the project-oriented nature of the work, they also may have to work evenings or weekends to meet deadlines or solve unexpected technical problems. Like other workers who sit for hours at a computer, typing on a keyboard, software engineers are susceptible to eyestrain, back discomfort and hand and wrist problems such as carpal tunnel syndrome.

As they strive to improve software for users, many computer software engineers interact with customers and coworkers. Computer software engineers who are employed by software vendors and consulting firms, for example, spend much of their time away from their offices, frequently travelling overnight to meet with customers. They call on customers in businesses ranging from manufacturing plants to financial institutions.

As networks expand, software engineers may be able to use modems, laptops, e-mail and the Internet to provide more technical support and other services from their main office, connecting to a customer's computer remotely to identify and correct developing problems.

Training, Other Qualifications and Advancement: Most employers prefer to hire persons who have at least a bachelor's degree and broad knowledge of and experience with, a variety of computer systems and technologies. The usual degree concentration for applications software engineers is computer science or software engineering; for systems software engineers, it is computer science or computer information systems. Graduate degrees are preferred for some of the more complex jobs.

Academic programmes in software engineering emphasize software and may be offered as a degree option or in conjunction with computer science degrees. Increasing emphasis on computer security suggests that software engineers with advanced degrees that include mathematics and systems design will be sought after by software developers, government agencies and consulting firms specializing in information assurance and security. Students seeking software engineering jobs enhance their employment opportunities by participating in internship or co-op programmes offered through their schools.

These experiences provide the students with broad knowledge and experience, making them more attractive candidates to employers. Inexperienced college graduates may be hired by large computer and consulting firms that train new employees in intensive, company-based programmes. In many firms, new hires are mentored and their mentors have an input into the performance evaluations of these new employees.

For systems software engineering jobs that require workers who have a college degree, a bachelor's degree in computer science or computer information systems is typical. For systems engineering jobs that place less emphasis on workers having a computer-related degree, computer training programmes leading to certification are offered by systems software vendors. Nonetheless, most training authorities feel that programme certification alone is not sufficient for the majority of software engineering jobs.

Persons interested in jobs as computer software engineers must have strong problem-solving and analytical skills. They also must be able to communicate effectively with team members, other staff and the customers they meet. Because they often deal with a number of tasks simultaneously, they must be able to concentrate and pay close attention to detail.

As is the case with most occupations, advancement opportunities for computer software engineers increase with experience. Entry-level computer software engineers are likely to test and verify ongoing designs.

As they become more experienced, they may become involved in designing and developing software. Eventually, they may advance to become a project manager, manager of information systems, or chief information officer. Some computer software engineers with several years of experience or expertise find lucrative opportunities working as systems designers or independent consultants or starting their own computer consulting firms.

As technological advances in the computer field continue, employers demand new skills. Computer software engineers must continually strive to acquire such skills if they wish to remain in this extremely dynamic field. For example, computer software engineers interested in working for a bank should have some expertise in finance as they integrate new technologies into the computer system of the bank. To help them keep up with the changing technology, continuing education and professional development seminars are offered by employers, software vendors, colleges and universities, private training institutions and professional computing societies.

Employment: Computer software engineers held about 800,000 jobs in 2004. Approximately 460,000 were computer applications software engineers and around 340,000 were computer systems software engineers. Although they are employed in most industries, the largest concentration of computer software engineers—almost 30 percent—are in computer systems design and related services. Many computer software engineers also work for establishments in other industries, such as software publishers, government agencies, manufacturers of computers and related electronic equipment and management of companies and enterprises.

Employers of computer software engineers range from start-up companies to established industry leaders. The proliferation of Internet, e-mail and other communications systems is expanding electronics to engineering firms that are traditionally associated with unrelated disciplines. Engineering firms specializing in building bridges and powerplants, for example, hire computer software engineers to design and develop new geographic data systems and automated drafting systems. Communications firms need computer software engineers to tap into growth in the personal communications market. Major communications companies have many job openings for both computer software applications engineers and computer systems engineers. An increasing number of computer software engineers are employed on a temporary or contract basis, with many being self-employed, working independently as consultants. Some consultants work for firms that specialize in developing and maintaining client companies' Web sites and intranets. About 23,000 computer software engineers were self-employed in 2004.

Job Outlook: Computer software engineers are projected to be one of the fastest-growing occupations from 2004 to 2014. Rapid employment growth in the computer systems design and related services industry, which employs the greatest number of computer software engineers, should result in very good opportunities for those college graduates with at least a bachelor's degree in computer engineering or computer science and practical experience working with computers. Employers will continue to seek computer professionals with strong programming, systems analysis, interpersonal and business skills. With the software industry beginning to mature, however and with routine software engineering work being increasingly outsourced overseas, job growth will not be as rapid as during the previous decade.

Employment of computer software engineers is expected to increase much faster than the average for all occupations, as businesses and other organizations adopt and integrate new technologies and seek to maximize the efficiency of their computer systems. Competition among businesses will continue to create an incentive for increasingly sophisticated technological innovations and organizations will need more computer software engineers to implement these changes. In addition to jobs created through employment growth, many job openings will result annually from the need to replace workers who move into managerial positions, transfer to other occupations, or leave the labour force.

Demand for computer software engineers will increase as computer networking continues to grow. For example, the expanding integration of Internet technologies and the explosive growth in electronic commerce—doing business on the Internet—have resulted in rising demand for computer software engineers who can develop Internet, intranet and World Wide Web applications. Likewise, expanding electronic data-processing systems in business, telecommunications, government and other settings continue to become more sophisticated and complex.

Growing numbers of systems software engineers will be needed to implement, safeguard and update systems and resolve problems. Consulting opportunities for computer software engineers also should continue to grow as businesses seek help to manage, upgrade and customize their increasingly complicated computer systems.

New growth areas will continue to arise from rapidly evolving technologies. The increasing uses of the Internet, the proliferation of Web sites and mobile technology such as the wireless Internet have created a demand for a wide variety of new products. As individuals and businesses rely more on hand-held computers and wireless networks, it will be necessary to integrate current computer systems with this new, more mobile technology.

Also, information security concerns have given rise to new software needs. Concerns over "cybersecurity" should result in businesses and government continuing to invest heavily in software that protects their networks and vital electronic infrastructure from attack. The expansion of this technology in the next 10 years will lead to an increased need for computer engineers to design and develop the software and systems to run these new applications and integrate them into older systems.

As with other information technology jobs, employment growth of computer software engineers may be tempered somewhat as more software development is contracted out abroad. Firms may look to cut costs by shifting operations to lower wage foreign countries with highly educated workers who have strong technical skills. At the same time, jobs in software engineering are less prone to being sent abroad compared with jobs in other computer specialties, because the occupation requires innovation and intense research and development.

Earnings: Median annual earnings of computer applications software engineers who worked full time in May 2004 were about $74,980. The middle 50 percent earned between $59,130 and $92,130. The lowest 10 percent earned less than $46,520 and the highest 10 percent earned more than $113,830. Median annual earnings in the industries employing the largest numbers of computer applications software engineers in May 2004 were as follows:

Software publishers	$79,930
Management, scientific and technical consulting services	78,460
Computer systems design and related services	76,910
Management of companies and enterprises	70,520
Insurance carriers	68,440

Median annual earnings of computer systems software engineers who worked full time in May 2004 were about $79,740. The middle 50 percent earned between $63,150 and $98,220. The lowest 10 percent earned less than $50,420 and the highest 10 percent earned more than $118,350. Median annual earnings in the industries employing the largest numbers of computer systems software engineers in May 2004 are as follows:

Scientific research and development services	$91,390
Computer and peripheral equipment manufacturing	87,800
Software publishers	83,670
Computer systems design and related services	79,950
Wired telecommunications carriers	74,370

According to the National Association of Colleges and Employers, starting salary offers for graduates with a bachelor's degree in computer engineering averaged $52,464 in 2005; offers for those with a master's degree averaged $60,354. Starting salary offers for graduates with a bachelor's degree in computer science averaged $50,820.

According to Robert Half International, starting salaries for software engineers in software development ranged from $63,250 to $92,750 in 2005. For network engineers, starting salaries in 2005 ranged from $61,250 to $88,250.

Computer Systems Analysts

Significant Points: Employers generally prefer applicants who have at least a bachelor's degree in computer science, information science, or management information systems (MIS).

Employment is expected to increase much faster than the average as organizations continue to adopt increasingly sophisticated technologies.

Job prospects are favourable.

Nature of the Work: All organizations rely on computer and information technology to conduct business and operate more efficiently. The rapid spread of technology across all industries has generated a need for highly trained workers to help organizations incorporate new technologies. The tasks performed by workers known as computer systems analysts evolve rapidly, reflecting new areas of specialization or changes in technology, as well as the preferences and practices of employers.

Computer systems analysts solve computer problems and apply computer technology to meet the individual needs of an organization. They help an organization to realize the maximum benefit from its investment in equipment, personnel and business processes. Systems analysts may plan and develop new computer systems or devise ways to apply existing systems' resources to additional operations. They may design new systems, including both hardware and software, or add a new software application to harness more of the computer's power. Most systems analysts work with specific types of systems—for example, business, accounting, or financial systems, or scientific and engineering systems—that vary with the kind of organization. Some systems analysts also are known as *systems developers* or *systems architects*.

Systems analysts begin an assignment by discussing the systems problem with managers and users to determine its exact nature. Defining the goals of the system and dividing the solutions into individual steps and separate procedures, systems analysts use techniques such as structured analysis, data modelling, information engineering, mathematical model building, sampling and cost accounting to plan the system. They specify the inputs to be accessed by the system, design the processing steps and format the output to meet users' needs. They also may prepare cost-benefit and return-on-investment analyses to help management decide whether implementing the proposed technology will be financially feasible.

When a system is accepted, systems analysts determine what computer hardware and software will be needed to set the system up. They coordinate tests and observe the initial use of the system to ensure that it performs as planned. They prepare specifications, flow charts and process diagrams for computer programmers to follow; then, they work with programmers to "debug," or eliminate, errors from the system. Systems analysts who do more in-depth testing of products may be referred to as *software quality assurance analysts*. In addition to running tests, these individuals diagnose problems, recommend solutions and determine whether programme requirements have been met.

In some organizations, *programmer-analysts* design and update the software that runs a computer. Because they are responsible for both programming and systems analysis, these workers must be proficient in both areas.

As this dual proficiency becomes more commonplace, these analysts are increasingly working with databases, object-oriented programming languages, as well as client–server applications development and multimedia and Internet technology.

One obstacle associated with expanding computer use is the need for different computer systems to communicate with each other. Because of the importance of maintaining up-to-date information—accounting records, sales figures, or budget projections, for example—systems analysts work on making the computer systems within an organization, or among organizations, compatible so that information can be shared among them. Many systems analysts are involved with "networking," connecting all the computers internally—in an individual office, department, or establishment—or externally, because many organizations rely on e-mail or the Internet. A primary goal of networking is to allow users to retrieve data from a mainframe computer or a server and use it on their desktop computer.

Systems analysts must design the hardware and software to allow the free exchange of data, custom applications and the computer power to process it all. For example, analysts are called upon to ensure the compatibility of computing systems between and among businesses to facilitate electronic commerce.

Working Conditions: Computer systems analysts work in offices or laboratories in comfortable surroundings. They usually work about 40 hours a week—the same as many other professional or office workers do. However, evening or weekend work may be necessary to meet deadlines or solve specific problems. Given the technology available today, telecommuting is common for computer professionals. As networks expand, more work can be done from remote locations through modems, laptops, electronic mail and the Internet.

Like other workers who spend long periods in front of a computer terminal typing on a keyboard, computer systems analysts are susceptible to eyestrain, back discomfort and hand and wrist problems such as carpal tunnel syndrome or cumulative trauma disorder.

Training, Other Qualifications and Advancement: Rapidly changing technology requires an increasing level of skill and education on the part of employees. Companies increasingly look for professionals with a broad background and range of skills, including not only technical knowledge, but also communication and other interpersonal skills. This shift from requiring workers to possess solely sound technical knowledge emphasizes workers who can handle various responsibilities.

While there is no universally accepted way to prepare for a job as a systems analyst, most employers place a premium on some formal college education. Relevant work experience also is very important. For more technically complex jobs, persons with graduate degrees are preferred.

Many employers seek applicants who have at least a bachelor's degree in computer science, information science, or management information systems (MIS). MIS programmes usually are part of the business school or college and differ considerably from computer science programmes, emphasizing business and management-oriented course work and business computing courses. Employers are increasingly seeking individuals with a master's degree in business administration (MBA), with a concentration in information systems, as more firms move their business to the Internet.

Despite employers' preference for those with technical degrees, persons with degrees in a variety of majors find employment as system analysts. The level of education and type of training that employers require depend on their needs. One factor affecting these needs is changes in technology. Employers often scramble to find workers capable of implementing "hot" new technologies such as the wireless Internet. Those workers with formal education or experience in information security, for example, are in demand because of the growing need for their skills and services. Another factor driving employers' needs is the timeframe during which a project must be completed.

Employers usually look for people who have broad knowledge and experience related to computer systems and technologies, strong problem-solving and analytical skills and good interpersonal skills. Courses in computer science or systems design offer good preparation for a job in these computer occupations. For jobs in a business environment, employers usually want systems analysts to have business management or closely related skills, while a background in the physical sciences, applied mathematics, or engineering is preferred for work in scientifically oriented organizations.

Job seekers can enhance their employment opportunities by participating in internship or co-op programmes offered through their schools. Because many people develop advanced computer skills in a non-computer-related occupation and then transfer those skills to a computer occupation, a background in the industry in which the person's job is located, such as financial services, banking, or accounting, can be important. Others have taken computer science courses to supplement their study in fields such as accounting, inventory control, or other business areas.

Computer systems analysts must be able to think logically and have good communication skills. Because they often deal with a number of tasks simultaneously, the ability to concentrate and pay close attention to detail is important. Although these workers sometimes work independently, they frequently work in teams on large projects. They must be able to communicate effectively with computer personnel, such as programmers and managers, as well as with users or other staff who may have no technical computer background.

Systems analysts may be promoted to senior or lead systems analyst. Those who show leadership ability also can become project managers or advance into management positions such as manager of information systems or chief information officer. Workers with work experience and considerable expertise in a particular subject or a certain application may find lucrative opportunities as independent consultants or may choose to start their own computer consulting firms.

Technological advances come so rapidly in the computer field that continuous study is necessary to keep one's skills up to date. Employers, hardware and software vendors, colleges and universities and private training institutions offer continuing education. Additional training may come from professional development seminars offered by professional computing societies.

Employment: Computer systems analysts held about 487,000 jobs in 2004; about 28,000 were self-employed.

Although they are increasingly employed in every sector of the economy, the greatest concentration of these workers is in the computer systems design and related services industry. Firms in this industry provide services related to the commercial use of computers on a contract basis, including custom computer programming services; computer systems integration design services; computer facilities management services, including computer systems or data processing facilities support services for clients; and other computer services, such as disaster recovery services and software installation. Computer systems analysts are also employed by governments, insurance companies, financial institutions, Internet service providers, data processing services firms and universities.

A growing number of systems analysts are employed on a temporary or contract basis; many of these individuals are self-employed, working independently as contractors or consultants. For example, a company installing a new computer system may need the services of several systems analysts just to get the system running. Because not all of the analysts would be needed once the system is functioning, the company might contract for such employees with a temporary help agency or a consulting firm or with the systems analysts themselves.

Such jobs may last from several months up to 2 years or more. This growing practice enables companies to bring in people with the exact skills the firm needs to complete a particular project, rather than having to spend time or money training or retraining existing workers. Often, experienced consultants then train a company's in-house staff as a project develops.

Job Outlook: Employment of computer systems analysts is expected to grow much faster than the average for all occupations through the year 2014 as organizations continue to adopt and integrate increasingly sophisticated technologies. Job increases will be driven by very rapid growth in computer system design and related services, which is projected to be among the fastest growing industries in the U.S. economy. In addition, many job openings will arise annually from the need to replace workers who move into managerial positions or other occupations or who leave the labour force. Job growth will not be as rapid as during the previous decade, however, as the information technology sector begins to mature and as routine work is increasingly outsourced to lower-wage foreign countries.

Workers in the occupation should enjoy favourable job prospects. The demand for networking to facilitate the sharing of information, the expansion of client–server environments and the need for computer specialists to use their knowledge and skills in a problem-solving capacity will be major factors in the rising demand for computer systems analysts. Moreover, falling prices of computer hardware and software should continue to induce more businesses to expand their computerized operations and integrate new technologies into them. In order to maintain a competitive edge and operate more efficiently, firms will keep demanding system analysts who are knowledgeable about the latest technologies and are able to apply them to meet the needs of businesses.

Increasingly, more sophisticated and complex technology is being implemented across all organizations, which should fuel the demand for these computer occupations. There is a growing demand for system analysts to help firms maximize their efficiency with available technology. Expansion of electronic commerce—doing business on the Internet—and the continuing need to build and maintain databases that store critical information on customers, inventory and projects are fuelling demand for database administrators familiar with the latest technology. Also, the increasing importance being placed on "cybersecurity"—the protection of electronic information—will result in a need for workers skilled in information security.

The development of new technologies usually leads to demand for various kinds of workers. The expanding integration of Internet technologies into businesses, for example, has resulted in a growing need for specialists who can develop and support Internet and intranet applications.

The growth of electronic commerce means that more establishments use the Internet to conduct their business online. The introduction of the wireless Internet, known as WiFi, creates new systems to be analyzed. The spread of such new technologies translates into a need for information technology professionals who can help organizations use technology to communicate with employees, clients and consumers. Explosive growth in these areas also is expected to fuel demand for analysts who are knowledgeable about network, data and communications security.

As technology becomes more sophisticated and complex, employers demand a higher level of skill and expertise from their employees. Individuals with an advanced degree in computer science or computer engineering, or with an MBA with a concentration in information systems, should enjoy favourable employment prospects. College graduates with a bachelor's degree in computer science, computer engineering, information science, or MIS also should enjoy favourable prospects for employment, particularly if they have supplemented their formal education with practical experience.

Because employers continue to seek computer specialists who can combine strong technical skills with good interpersonal and business skills, graduates with non-computer-science degrees, but who have had courses in computer programming, systems analysis and other information technology subjects, also should continue to find jobs in computer fields. In fact, individuals with the right experience and training can work in computer occupations regardless of their college major or level of formal education.

Earnings: Median annual earnings of computer systems analysts were $66,460 in May 2004. The middle 50 percent earned between $52,400 and $82,980 a year. The lowest 10 percent earned less than $41,730 and the highest 10 percent earned more than $99,180. Median annual earnings in the industries employing the largest numbers of computer systems analysts in May 2004 were:

Federal Government	$71,770
Computer systems design and related services	69,560
Management of companies and enterprises	67,230
Insurance carriers	66,840
State government	57,040

According to the National Association of Colleges and Employers, starting offers for graduates with a master's degree in computer science averaged $62,727 in 2005. Starting offers averaged $50,820 for graduates with a bachelor's degree in computer science; $46,189 for those with a degree in computer systems analysis; $44,417 for those with a degree in management information systems; and $44,775 for those with a degree in information sciences and systems.

According to Robert Half International, starting salaries for systems analysts ranged from $61,500 to $82,500 in 2005.

Computer Scientists and Database Administrators

Significant Points: Education requirements range from an associate degree to a doctoral degree.

Employment is expected to increase much faster than the average as organizations continue to adopt increasingly sophisticated technologies.

Job prospects are favourable.

Nature of the Work: The rapid spread of computers and information technology has generated a need for highly trained workers proficient in various job functions. These workers—computer scientists, database administrators and network systems and data communication analysts—include a wide range of computer specialists. Job tasks and occupational titles used to describe these workers evolve rapidly, reflecting new areas of specialization or changes in technology, as well as the preferences and practices of employers.

Computer scientists work as theorists, researchers, or inventors. Their jobs are distinguished by the higher level of theoretical expertise and innovation they apply to complex problems and the creation or application of new technology. Those employed by academic institutions work in areas ranging from complexity theory to hardware to programming-language design. Some work on multidisciplinary projects, such as developing and advancing uses of virtual reality, extending human-computer interaction, or designing robots. Their counterparts in private industry work in areas such as applying theory; developing specialized languages or information technologies; or designing programming tools, knowledge-based systems, or even computer games.

With the Internet and electronic business generating large volumes of data, there is a growing need to be able to store, manage and extract data effectively. *Database administrators* work with database management systems software and determine ways to organize and store data. They identify user requirements, set up computer databases and test and coordinate modifications to the computer database systems. An organization's database administrator ensures the performance of the system, understands the platform on which the database runs and adds new users to the system. Because they also may design and implement system security, database administrators often plan and coordinate security measures. With the volume of sensitive data generated every second growing rapidly, data integrity, backup systems and database security have become increasingly important aspects of the job of database administrators.

Because networks are configured in many ways, *network systems and data communications analysts* are needed to design, test and evaluate systems such as local area networks (LANs), wide area networks (WANs), the Internet, intranets and other data communications systems. Systems can range from a connection between two offices in the same building to globally distributed networks, voice mail and e-mail systems of a multinational organization. Network systems and data communications analysts perform network modelling, analysis and planning; they also may research related products and make necessary hardware and software recommendations. *Telecommunications specialists* focus on the interaction between computer and communications equipment. These workers design voice and data communication systems, supervise the installation of the systems and provide maintenance and other services to clients after the systems are installed.

The growth of the Internet and the expansion of the World Wide Web (the graphical portion of the Internet) have generated a variety of occupations related to the design, development and maintenance of Web sites and their servers. For example, *webmasters* are responsible for all technical aspects of a Web site, including performance issues such as speed of access and for approving the content of the site. *Internet developers* or *Web developers*, also called *Web designers*, are responsible for day-to-day site creation and design.

Working Conditions: Computer scientists and database administrators normally work in offices or laboratories in comfortable surroundings. They usually work about 40 hours a week—the same as many other professional or office workers do. However, evening or weekend work may be necessary to meet deadlines or solve specific problems. With the technology available today, telecommuting is common for computer professionals. As networks expand, more work can be done from remote locations through modems, laptops, electronic mail and the Internet.

Like other workers who spend long periods in front of a computer terminal typing on a keyboard, computer scientists and database administrators are susceptible to eyestrain, back discomfort and hand and wrist problems such as carpal tunnel syndrome or cumulative trauma disorder.

Training, Other Qualifications and Advancement: Rapidly changing technology requires an increasing level of skill and education on the part of employees. Companies look for professionals with an ever-broader background and range of skills, including not only technical knowledge, but also communication and other interpersonal skills. While there is no universally accepted way to prepare for a job as a network systems analyst, computer scientist, or database administrator, most employers place a premium on some formal college education. A bachelor's degree is a prerequisite for many jobs; however, some jobs may require only a 2-year degree. Relevant work experience also is very important. For more technically complex jobs, persons with graduate degrees are preferred.

For database administrator positions, many employers seek applicants who have a bachelor's degree in computer science, information science, or management information systems (MIS). MIS programmes usually are part of the business school or college and differ considerably from computer science programmes, emphasizing business and management-oriented coursework and business computing courses. Employers increasingly seek individuals with a master's degree in business administration (MBA), with a concentration in information systems, as more firms move their business to the Internet. For some network systems and data communication analysts, such as webmasters, an associate degree or certificate is sufficient, although more advanced positions might require a computer-related bachelor's degree. For computer and information scientists, a doctoral degree generally is required because of the highly technical nature of their work.

Despite employers' preference for those with technical degrees, persons with degrees in a variety of majors find employment in these occupations. The level of education and the type of training that employers require depend on their needs. One factor affecting these needs is changes in technology. Employers often scramble to find workers capable of implementing new technologies. Workers with formal education or experience in information security, for example, are in demand because of the growing need for their skills and services. Employers also look for workers skilled in wireless technologies as wireless networks and applications have spread into many firms and organizations.

Most community colleges and many independent technical institutes and proprietary schools offer an associate's degree in computer science or a related information technology field. Many of these programmes may be geared more toward meeting the needs of local businesses and are more occupation specific than are 4-year degree programmes. Some jobs may be better suited to the level of training that such programmes offer. Employers usually look for people who have broad knowledge and experience related to computer systems and technologies, strong problem-solving and analytical skills and good interpersonal skills. Courses in computer science or systems design offer good preparation for a job in these computer occupations. For jobs in a business environment, employers usually want systems analysts to have business management or closely related skills, while a background in the physical sciences, applied mathematics, or engineering is preferred for work in scientifically oriented organizations. Art or graphic design skills may be desirable for webmasters or Web developers.

Jobseekers can enhance their employment opportunities by participating in internship or co-op programmes offered through their schools. Because many people develop advanced computer skills in a non-computer occupation and then transfer those skills to a computer occupation, a background in the industry in which the person's job is located, such as financial services, banking, or accounting, can be important. Others have taken computer science courses to supplement their study in fields such as accounting, inventory control, or other business areas.

Computer scientists and database administrators must be able to think logically and have good communication skills. Because they often deal with a number of tasks simultaneously, the ability to concentrate and pay close attention to detail is important. Although these computer specialists sometimes work independently, they frequently work in teams on large projects. They must be able to communicate effectively with computer personnel, such as programmers and managers, as well as with users or other staff who may have no technical computer background.

Computer scientists employed in private industry may advance into managerial or project leadership positions. Those employed in academic institutions can become heads of research departments or published authorities in their field. Database administrators may advance into managerial positions, such as chief technology officer, on the basis of their experience managing data and enforcing security. Computer specialists with work experience and considerable expertise in a particular subject or a certain application may find lucrative opportunities as independent consultants or may choose to start their own computer consulting firms.

Technological advances come so rapidly in the computer field that continuous study is necessary to keep one's skills up to date. Employers, hardware and software vendors, colleges and universities and private training institutions offer continuing education. Additional training may come from professional development seminars offered by professional computing societies.

Certification is a way to demonstrate a level of competence in a particular field. Some product vendors or software firms offer certification and require professionals who work with their products to be certified. Many employers regard these certifications as the industry standard. For example, one method of acquiring enough knowledge to get a job as a database administrator is to become certified in a specific type of database management. Voluntary certification also is available through various organizations associated with computer specialists. Professional certification may afford a jobseeker a competitive advantage.

Employment: Computer scientists and database administrators held about 507,000 jobs in 2004, including about 66,000 who were self-employed. Employment was distributed among the detailed occupations as follows:

Network systems and data communication analysts	231,000
Database administrators	104,000
Computer and information scientists, research	22,000
Computer specialists, all other	149,000

Although they are increasingly employed in every sector of the economy, the greatest concentration of these workers is in the computer systems design and related services industry. Firms in this industry provide services related to the commercial use of computers on a contract basis, including custom computer programming services; computer systems integration design services; computer facilities management services, including computer systems or data processing facilities support services for clients; and other computer-related services, such as disaster recovery services and software installation.

Many computer scientists and database administrators are employed by Internet service providers; Web search portals; and data processing, hosting and related services firms. Others work for government, manufacturers of computer and electronic products, insurance companies, financial institutions and universities.

A growing number of computer specialists, such as network and data communications analysts, are employed on a temporary or contract basis; many of these individuals are self-employed, working independently as contractors or consultants. For example, a company installing a new computer system may need the services of several network systems and data communication analysts just to get the system running. Because not all of the analysts would be needed once the system is functioning, the company might contract for such employees with a temporary help agency or a consulting firm or with the network systems analysts themselves.

Such jobs may last from several months to 2 years or more. This growing practice enables companies to bring in people with the exact skills they need to complete a particular project, rather than having to spend time or money training or retraining existing workers. Often, experienced consultants then train a company's in-house staff as a project develops.

Job Outlook: Computer scientists and database administrators should continue to enjoy favourable job prospects. As technology becomes more sophisticated and complex, however, employers demand a higher level of skill and expertise from their employees. Individuals with an advanced degree in computer science or computer engineering or with an MBA with a concentration in information systems should enjoy favourable employment prospects. College graduates with a bachelor's degree in computer science, computer engineering, information science, or MIS also should enjoy favourable prospects, particularly if they have supplemented their formal education with practical experience.

Because employers continue to seek computer specialists who can combine strong technical skills with good interpersonal and business skills, graduates with degrees in fields other than computer science who have had courses in computer programming, systems analysis and other information technology areas also should continue to find jobs in these computer fields. In fact, individuals with the right experience and training can work in these computer occupations regardless of their college major or level of formal education.

Computer scientists and database administrators are expected to be among the fastest growing occupations through 2014. Employment of these computer specialists is expected to grow much faster than the average for all occupations as organizations continue to adopt and integrate increasingly sophisticated technologies. Job increases will be driven by very rapid growth in computer systems design and related services, which is projected to be one of the fastest growing industries in the U.S. economy.

Job growth will not be as rapid as during the previous decade, however, as the information technology sector begins to mature and as routine work is increasingly outsourced overseas. In addition to growth, many job openings will arise annually from the need to replace workers who move into managerial positions or other occupations or who leave the labour force.

The demand for networking to facilitate the sharing of information, the expansion of client–server environments and the need for computer specialists to use their knowledge and skills in a problem-solving capacity will be major factors in the rising demand for computer scientists and database administrators. Moreover, falling prices of computer hardware and software should continue to induce more businesses to expand their computerized operations and integrate new technologies into them. To maintain a competitive edge and operate more efficiently, firms will keep demanding computer specialists who are knowledgeable about the latest technologies and are able to apply them to meet the needs of businesses.

Increasingly, more sophisticated and complex technology is being implemented across all organizations, fuelling demand for computer scientists and database administrators. There is growing demand for network systems and data communication analysts to help firms maximize their efficiency with available technology.

Expansion of electronic commerce—doing business on the Internet—and the continuing need to build and maintain databases that store critical information on customers, inventory and projects are fuelling demand for database administrators familiar with the latest technology. Also, the increasing importance placed on cybersecurity—the protection of electronic information—will result in a need for workers skilled in information security.

The development of new technologies usually leads to demand for various kinds of workers. The expanding integration of Internet technologies into businesses, for example, has resulted in a growing need for specialists who can develop and support Internet and intranet applications. The growth of electronic commerce means that more establishments use the Internet to conduct their business online. The introduction of the wireless Internet, known as WiFi, creates new systems to be analyzed and new data to be administered. The spread of such new technologies translates into a need for information technology professionals who can help organizations use technology to communicate with employees, clients and consumers. Explosive growth in these areas also is expected to fuel demand for specialists who are knowledgeable about network, data and communications security.

Earnings: Median annual earnings of computer and information scientists, research, were $85,190 in May 2004. The middle 50 percent earned between $64,860 and $108,440. The lowest 10 percent earned less than $48,930 and the highest 10 percent earned more than $132,700. Median annual earnings of computer and information scientists employed in computer systems design and related services in May 2004 were $85,530.

Median annual earnings of database administrators were $60,650 in May 2004. The middle 50 percent earned between $44,490 and $81,140. The lowest 10 percent earned less than $33,380 and the highest 10 percent earned more than $97,450. In May 2004, median annual earnings of database administrators employed in computer systems design and related services were $70,530 and for those in management of companies and enterprises, earnings were $65,990.

Median annual earnings of network systems and data communication analysts were $60,600 in May 2004. The middle 50 percent earned between $46,480 and $78,060. The lowest 10 percent earned less than $36,260 and the highest 10 percent earned more than $95,040. Median annual earnings in the industries employing the largest numbers of network systems and data communications analysts in May 2004 are shown below:

Wired telecommunications carriers	$65,130
Insurance carriers	64,660
Management of companies and enterprises	64,170
Computer systems design and related services	63,910
Local government	52,300

Median annual earnings of all other computer specialists were $59,480 in May 2004. Median annual earnings of all other computer specialists employed in computer systems design and related services were $57,430 and, for those in management of companies and enterprises, earnings were $68,590 in May 2004.

According to the National Association of Colleges and Employers, starting offers for graduates with a doctoral degree in computer science averaged $93,050 in 2005. Starting offers averaged $50,820 for graduates with a bachelor's degree in computer science; $46,189 for those with a degree in computer systems analysis; $44,417 for those with a degree in management information systems; and $44,775 for those with a degree in information sciences and systems.

According to Robert Half International, a firm providing specialized staffing services, starting salaries in 2005 ranged from $67,750 to $95,500 for database administrators. Salaries for networking and Internet-related occupations ranged from $47,000 to $68,500 for LAN administrators and from $51,750 to $74,520 for web developers. Starting salaries for information security professionals ranged from $63,750 to $93,000 in 2005.

2

Career in Information Technology

Information Technology Industry

If you are considering a career in Information Technology (IT), you'll soon realize that there are many occupations available and that IT careers give you the flexibility to work in many different industries.

Just look around and you can see how much we rely on technology everyday. Imagine being part of this exciting, growing and changing industry. IT remains a critical aspect of work in all industries and sectors, as well as an industry in its own right. However, America continues to suffer from a shortage of qualified IT workers with flexible and portable skills who can readily adapt and respond to ever-changing IT demands and processes.

If you do decide to specialize in technology, you should know that the industry can be viewed either by the types of jobs available or by the industries which are technology driven.

Technology skills and computer proficiency are essential assets for workers in all industries. Even if the career you choose does not focus solely on IT, the job will most likely require the use of computers and technology to accomplish tasks and process information. 92% of all IT workers are in non-IT companies, 80% of which are in small companies (Information Technology Association of America).

For all IT-related occupations, technical and professional certifications are growing more popular and increasingly important. IT workers must continually update and acquire new skills to remain qualified in this dynamic field. Completion of vocational training also is an asset. According to a May 2000 report by the Urban Institute, community colleges play a critical role in training new workers and in retraining both veteran workers and workers from other fields.

People interested in becoming computer support specialists generally need only an Associate degree in a computer-related field, as well as significant hands-on experience with computers. They also must possess strong problem-solving and analytical skills as well as excellent communication skills because troubleshooting and helping others are such vital aspects of the job. And because there is constant interaction on the job with other computer personnel, customers and employees, computer support specialists must be able to communicate effectively on paper, using e-mail and in person. They also must possess strong writing skills when preparing manuals for employees and customers.

From the basic entry level positions to Chief Information Officers, there are almost limitless possibilities in Information Technology.

Do you want a rewarding career in a growing industry? Do you want higher pay and benefits and opportunities for advanced education and training?

Constant change defines the Information Technology (IT) industry. Many occupations in the industry that are commonplace today didn't exist even a decade ago. There is a gap between the education and skill levels of the existing IT workforce and the proficiency desired by employers. Education and credentials help individuals gain entry into many occupations; however, experience and training are essential for high performance.

A Career in Information Technology (IT)

Considering a career in IT is a little like negotiating the M25—there are many ways in, it can be confusing and there are different opinions as to the best route—but once you've found your route it is very satisfying. One of the things that can make an IT career both exciting and daunting is the fact that there is an increasing rate of change in all areas of the field. This can make some skills irrelevant very quickly or over-emphasise others, so a well informed choice requires research.

There are numerous employment areas: quality management and standards, education and training, research, software testing, database design, configuration and change management, systems development, web design and so on.

Despite the bad publicity caused by the dot.com crashes of the past few years there are still rewarding careers to be had in IT—temporary slumps in IT recruitment are just that—temporary. Why? Because IT permeates every aspect of our lives and our lives can literally depend on it, which is why after September 11 the issues of risk management and business continuity have been brought to the fore in the business and IT press—and they are interesting and vital professions.

In fact, even if you don't pursue a career in IT specifically, you will still need IT skills. Whether you become a bus driver, an administrator, a doctor, a writer, a meter reader...whatever, IT skills are needed in the 21st century.

In the IT arena itself many are initially attracted by their love of technology from youth—often fostered by science fiction films, books or magazines. The cutting edge of IT today is an exciting place, so let's look at some examples.

Following a slump in interest in the 1980s, apart from in the chess playing computer Deep Blue, organisations began exploiting the commercial possibilities of Artificial Intelligence (AI). This has quickly led to speech recognition software and the 'intelligent agents' in web browsers.

Contemporary AI applications include Microsoft's Natural Language Processing Group—which is working on enabling people to instruct computers in plain language and has led to the grammar checker in MS Office. US corporation Cycorp have been compiling a database of 'rules', on the premise that given enough direction a computer will become capable of reasoning. Their technology has been successfully applied to a network security system.

In the opening story of Ray Bradbury's The Illustrated Man two children become obsessed with a room which synthesises 'real' environments; an adventurous portrayal at the time of a virtual reality. In today's cultural lexicon, though, there is no surprise in the idea of virtual worlds, the concept of 'avatars'—virtual representations of individuals—or the act of interacting with a computer generated environment.

The underlying premise of VR today is to create fuller methods for human-computer interaction—there is much more to VR than 3-D entertainment.

A potentially very rewarding VR career area could be in the science of haptics—systems that create physical sensations via force feedback for VR applications. In the medical world haptics can take the form of a force feedback assembly to help train surgeons—vital in a job where it is not only sight but the feeling of making incisions and the pressure required in different circumstances that are needed.

In the entertainment world VR experts are aiming for total submersion interactivity—The Matrix beckons.

What about 'Robotics', a term coined by writer and scientist Isaac Asimov, most famously in I Robot (1950) a collection of short stories that based their plots around contradictions in the 'Three Laws of Robotics'?

When robots were first used in industry in the 1950's it seemed that the vision of human facsimiles would remain unfulfilled. However, recently the humanoid robot has made a comeback courtesy of Honda Motor Company. In February 2002 the company celebrated the 25th anniversary of its listing on the New York Stock Exchange by having ASIMO, the world's most advanced humanoid robot, ring the opening bell for trading.

Honda's research was undertaken with the aim of developing a new type of robot that would be used in daily life, rather than a robot purpose-built for special operations.

ASIMO (Advanced Step in Innovative Mobility) is a people-friendly 120cm-tall machine that is able to perform tasks within the realm of the human environment. The latest version walks freely, climbs and descends stairways and slopes and has a top speed of 2 km per hour.

It has an onboard voice recognition function and it is possible to use voice commands to control its arm and hand motions and locomotion. It can even recognize the direction of a sound source, enabling it to face the direction of its operators' voice and follow their commands.

ASIMO robots are being leased to several corporations and museums for use in greeting people at offices and events and recently one started working as a receptionist for visitors to Honda's Aoyama Headquarters—although its salary is yet to be divulged.

The foregoing projects have the input of a multitude of IT areas from specialists in software development to the engineers to the project managers. These examples demonstrate that IT is such a diverse industry that there are a wide range of training and qualification paths—so narrowing down your area of interest may be an important first step in deciding on your route. However, if at a later date you decide to refocus your career aims, there will always be a way in for those who have a good grounding in another area of IT.

Information Technology Careers and Information

What is Information Technology: Information technology, IT is usually involved in the context of a business and is often used to automate manual tasks as well as improve efficiencies within an organisation. By involving computer systems, IT has helped industry reach new markets and apply new services to customers and clients.

Areas in Information Technology: In the developing information technology field their is a particular trend in specialisation . In partcular to databases, office information systems, local area networks (LANs), wide area networks (WANs), the internet and programming.

Computer Programming Information: Provides programming languages information including types of programming and types of examples of programming languages.

Introduction to Programming:: A computer cannot understand the words spoken by us and this warrants the need of a language, which can prompt the machine to carry the functions we desire. The pursuit of developing the perfect computer language, which started from the simple punched cards and algorithms, has taken a whole new dimension today.

The present day computer languages are immensely capable in making the computer perform varied tasks in fields like art, engineering, medical science etc. A complete programming language includes components like, the computational model, the syntax and semantics of programmes and the other pragmatic considerations that shape the language.

Programming Needs: Theré are different types of computer languages developed for different needs. A generic classification language types is as follows: Logic Programming, Functional Programming, Imperative Programming and Object orientated Programming.

Computer Programming: A programme is set of coded instructions that enable a machine, especially a computer, to perform a desired sequence of operations. Thus programming languages deal with such sets of instructions or algorithms, which can be customized according to the output, we desire from the computer. Some of the most prominent programming languages are as follows:

Computer Programming Jobs Provides information about computer programming jobs including types of programming, qualifications required and specializations.

What is Computer Programming?: Computer programming is the imputing of sequenced instructions that direct a computer to take assigned actions or determine logical steps.

What is a Computer Programmer: Computer programmers write, test and maintain the programmes that computers follow when performing specific functions. While job titles and descriptions vary by company, the main task of computer programmers is problem solving and development of systems solutions using the appropriate methodologies and techniques.

Programmers often work on projects as a team, each team member assigned according to strength and ability. A programmer uses programming languages, such as C++, PHP, or Java to communicate with computer to perform a set of instructions. By typing code in 2nd and 3rd level programming languages (which are languages become more like words as the generation goes up and more like machine code as the generation goes down, *e.g.* assembler) helps computer programmers easier to code with. Once finished coding they compile the programme into machine language so the computer can follow the set of instructions.

What Qualifications do Computer Programmers Need?

A Bachelor's degree in Computer Science is generally required for employment at the more prestigious technology companies. However, the combination of an associate's degree with strong computer programming ability will qualify programmers for many entry-level positions. Regardless of the degree chosen, courses in information science, computer science, mathematics and engineering provide the kind of strong base knowledge employers look for. Additional qualifications include:

- Certification in a specific programming language or languages
- Familiarity with database systems
- Good communication skills
- An eye for detail
- An ability to think "out of the box"
- An analytical mind and problem solving skills

What type of tasks are involved in Computer Programming?

In addition to writing new programmes, computer programmers update and maintain existing programmes. They test programmes to ensure efficiency, accuracy and to identify programming errors. Some of the tasks programmers might also do the following:

- Prepare computer operator instructions
- Work with field experts to create custom software

- Analyze technical data, designs and prototypes
- Prepare and present reports on project specifications, activities and status
- Write computer software, programmes, or code
- Document reliability of technical specifications
- Work with software providers to increase proficiencies while working within applications
- Work cross-departmental on development and support
- Prepare software documentation for end users

It is imperative that computer programmers stay informed and aware of changing technological trends and advances—which occur almost weekly in this progressive field.

Are there Areas of specialization?

Programmers may be applications or system programmers. Applications programmers write and revise programmes that work with specific software to handle a specific job.

Systems programmers create the operating software for entire systems that allow the recognition and use of operating systems; networked systems and database systems. Within these two categories are many specific specializations. Computer programmers can focus on the following areas or combine them for added marketability:

- Multimedia
- The Internet
- Specific computer languages
- Research
- Management

What types of companies employ Computer Programmers?

Computer programmers are needed in organizations that deal with large data processing components. The technology and software industry employs the largest percentage of computer programmers. However, they can be found in government, communications, pharmaceuticals and financial institutions.

Computer Engineers

Computer engineers design and test computer hardware and software.

Look around. There are computers everywhere. Well, of course. You see a lot of desktops inside office buildings. There's always someone with a laptop inside the local coffee house. But did you know there's a computer inside your VCR? Your car? Inside the x-ray machine at the hospital? The ATM? Cash registers?

Computer engineers are behind all these computers. They are part of a team of workers who develop computer equipment (hardware) and programmes (software). Computer engineers are the team members who solve theoretical problems. They apply their knowledge of math and science to computer design. They help solve technical problems and pass that information on to team members who do the programming or create the equipment. However, engineers sometimes are involved in the hands-on part of the job.

Regardless of whether they develop software or hardware, engineers have some tasks in common. Before starting a project, they talk to clients to find out more about their needs. They also learn about the time line, security needs and cost limitations. During projects, engineers test or supervise those who test their work. Once they complete projects, engineers may train clients how to use software or maintain hardware. They also monitor systems and repair those that are not functioning properly. Hardware and software engineers work together on some tasks. For example, they make sure that the hardware is able to handle the demands of the software.

Software engineers develop computer software systems, such as those that control manufacturing processes. They research, design and test all parts of the software. For example, they look at the current operating system and determine how the new software will work with it. These engineers have strong programming skills. However, they spend more time analyzing and solving programming problems than doing programming. They supervise workers who do much of the programming and documenting. Engineers examine work as it is completed and suggest modifications. When the software is finished, engineers coordinate its installation on the client's system.

Many hardware engineers are involved in the development of hardware such as computer chips. However, some hardware engineers put together systems that will handle clients' needs. After gathering information from clients, engineers determine the best way to upgrade or replace the client's current hardware. They make sure the system is installed in a good environment. Thus, they may recommend that clients purchase equipment that controls the dust and temperature in the computer area. They may also require clients to rewire the computer area so that computers have a stable power supply. Engineers supervise the installation of the system and monitor its performance.

COBOL Programming

COBOL is an acronym for 'Common Business Oriented Language'. It was written in the 1960s keeping the business applications in mind. The language has a simple structure, which uses English-like sentences and paragraphs. It was generally used to create programmes for the main frames in big business firms. COBOL was last upgraded in late 1999 when the Y2K problem surfaced.

The basic drawback of COBOL is its verbosity. Traditional COBOL programming will never be outdated, but will be gradually be complemented by new language features for defining classes and objects.

Types of Programming

Provides information the different types of programming including relevant reference sites.

1. *Logic Programming:* Logical Programming languages operate on facts and relationships from which they can draw a coherent and simple conclusion.
2. *Functional Programming:* Functional programming languages are more closely related to the mathematical concept of 'function' than imperative programming

languages. This makes it easier to apply programme-proving techniques and logical reasoning to functional programmes. In particular, functional programmes do not use the concept of variables in the traditional sense, *i.e.* a memory location whose contents might be changed from time to time as a programme executes.

3. *Imperative Programming:* Imperative programming is associated with languages like C, Fortran, Pascal etc. Imperative programming is distinguished from functional programming in that the former is strongly tied to the concept of variables and memory locations. A variable is associated with a memory location and the contents of that memory location may be changed, via the variable, over the course of time.

   The meaning or effect of a programme fragment at a particular point can only be understood by reference to the current contents of the set of relevant variables, therefore. In contrast, functional programmes do not allow the contents of a variable to be changed once set (in simplified terms), hence making them easier to reason about. While languages such as C++ and Java are also imperative programming languages, strictly speaking, they are more commonly referred to as object-oriented programming languages.

4. *Concurrent Programming:* Concurrent programming is characterized by programming with more than one process. The main advantage of concurrent programming is that operations can run parallel in it, thus they are much faster than sequential operations. Basically, concurrent programming uses processes and communication to design elegant, responsive and reliable systems.

5. *Object-Oriented Programming:* Object oriented programming is the method of implementing programmes which are organized as cooperative collections of objects and each of which represents an instance of some class and whose classes are all members of a hierarchy of classes united via inheritance relationships. In these types

of programmes, classes are generally viewed as static, whereas objects typically have a much more dynamic nature, which is encouraged by the existence of polymorphism.

Career Opportunities for Majors

The School of Communication, Information and Library Studies offers the major in Information Technology and Informatics. This programme emphasizes the evaluation, implementation and management of information technologies for a wide range of organizations. Information Technology and Informatics unites theories drawn from the humanities and social sciences with practical computer-based competencies. This combination prepares students to work in a diverse marketplace which demands individuals who understand the social and economic impact of technology locally and globally and the effective use of technology in organizations.

Information Technology and Informatics graduates find opportunities in a wide variety of careers in business, education, government and the non-profit sectors. The combination of technical skills and verbal/written communication skills is a desirable characteristic employers seek when hiring. Any work that involves communicating as its focal point is a potential career field. The information technology industry is a competitive one, however and experience is a must.

While most graduates work in a related occupation, others choose different directions. Experience has allowed some to progress without further education. However, an advanced degree can offer an edge, particularly with larger corporations. Many careers do not require a specific major but rather a wide range of demonstrated skills and accomplishments. Regardless of your career choices, increase your marketability to employers through internships, responsible work experience, good grades and involvement in college activities.

A Sample of Related Occupations

Computer Service Representative

Help Desk Analyst

Systems Consultant
Consultant
Human Resources Info. Specialist
Technical Analyst
Customer Support Coordinator
Information Officer
Technical Evaluator
Data Specialist
Instructional Technology Designer
Technical Researcher
Data Processing Manager
IT Specialist
Technical Writer
Database Administrator
Network Administrator
User Interface Specialist
Database Analyst
Project Manager
Web Analyst
Database Designer
Project Team Leader
Web Designer
Electronic Commerce Developer
Quality Assurance Analyst
Web Information Officer

Types of Employers

Private and Non-profit Organizations

Advertising Agencies
Management/Consulting Firms
Computer Firms
Manufacturing Firms

Community Organizations
Media Firms
Consulting Firms
Newspapers
Educational Organizations
Non-profit Organizations
Entertainment Firms
Pharmaceutical/Biotech Firms
Financial Institutions
Professional Associations
Health Organizations
Public Relations Firms
Hospitality Organizations
Publishing Companies
Hospitals
Radio Stations
Information Design Agencies
Research Organizations
Investment Firms
Telecommunications Firms
Labour Unions
Television Stations

Government Agencies

Central Intelligence Agency
General Accounting Office
Department of Commerce
National Archives
Department of Energy
National Science Foundation
Department of Labour
National Telecommunications and
Information Administration

Department of Treasury

Securities & Exchange Commission

FBI

Small Business Administration

Federal Retirement Thrift Investment Board

U.S. Information Agency

Federal Trade Commission

Jobs Obtained by Rutgers Graduates

Chief Information Officer, AOL Time Warner

IT Specialist, Picatinny Arsenal

Chief Technology Officer, Deutsche Bank (MBA—IT)

Lead Engineer, Motorola

Executive IT Support Specialist, Warner Music Group

Network Administrator, Musculoskeletal Transplant Foundation

Graduate Student, Rutgers University (MS Information Technology)

Quality Assurance Analyst, RTTS

Information Services Leadership Programme, J&J

SAP Help Desk Analyst, KForce

Web Designer, Rutgers University

Directory of Canadian IT Companies

IT Careers Canada provides you a pertinent and accurate list of Information Technology companies listed alphabetically.

Many Information Technology companies promise their employees career mobility and opportunities within, to grow professionally and remain employable.

Regardless of how much a company support it's employees professional development, IT employees need to realize it is their career and ultimately their responsibility.

Only few positions are filled through Internet conventional job boards. Job seekers should research a more modern approach.

IT Careers Canada assists you to directly access a Canadian company through the career opportunity page or, the main entry page.

You will gain time using IT Careers Canada as your start page to focus on the IT jobs you are searching for.

IT Job Opportunities—IT Job Postings

As an added value service, IT Careers Canada, by partnering with Brainhunter's solution of technology, is proud to offer IT JOB SEEKERS and IT EMPLOYERS, the hub of the most advanced network of CareerSites on the web.

Job Seekers: The service is absolutely FREE for you and offers access to unique job opportunities within your information technology. Employers can visit your site and find specific skill sets and available, interested candidates:

- Secure and confidential job seeker account
- Customized job search agents
- Store up to 3 unique profiles

Employers: You will enjoy posting positions to the CareerSite and receiving only qualified industry specific job seekers / candidates to your open positions. CareerSite provides employers Quality over Quantity:

- Direct access to qualified candidates within your community
- Secure Job Management allows you to post, edit and delete jobs at any time
- Automatic pre-screening of candidates into "A" lists and "B" lists
- A unique Resume database customized specifically to your niche industry.

IT Careers Canada invites IT JOB SEEKERS and IT EMPLOYERS to experiment this great opportunity.

Canadian IT Publications

Canada's ultimate IT source for business with up to date news, interviews, product information and online community for the Canadian information technology professional.

Professional Services: The professional services category encompasses everything from software programming, consulting, to training. Careers in this sector focus on assisting companies install and utilize computer technology based on their specific needs.

Today, a great demand exists for workers with a strong understanding of the Internet, intranets and web-based application design. People with skills in Java programming, security and firewall expertise and the ability to connect presentation level interfaces, databases and legacy systems are also in demand.

According to the U.S. Bureau of Labour Statistics, computer programming professionals often receive ongoing education and training in new technologies. More programmers are needed in software maintenance than in software development and these maintenance programmers must be familiar with many types of hardware and software. They need to understand the Internet and networking technology and also possess the ability to work as development programmers.

Many employers are interested in technical staff who have a strong understanding of prevailing computer languages and technologies in their field and who are willing to quickly develop new skills, as corporate needs change. Programmers with broad training and in-depth knowledge of several fields have the greatest potential for success.

Individuals with these skills usually work for commercial and government clients and produce unique computer systems based an on organization's specified requirements. They conduct tasks in various phases of a system's life cycle including planning, designing, constructing, implementing and operating.

This particular IT sector is rapidly expanding due to advancing technology, a shortage of technical personnel and the constantly evolving requirements of business.

Processing Services: IT processing services specializes in electronic recordkeeping, transaction processing and information retrieval. Careers in this category focus on software and hardware development as well as systems maintenance. These services include payroll processing, consumer data collection and storage and e-commerce transactions. Professionals in information services also create, update and analyze the vast stores of vital and proprietary data that may lead to a revolutionary service or give their organization a crucial competitive advantage.

Computer programmers, system analysts, information processing and delivery professionals, are all processing services occupations. Sales representatives, administrative personnel, writers and editors and research analysts are all occupations that also depend upon and make use of information processing services.

Careers in Information Systems

Undergraduate Career Information: There has been and continues to be high demand for well-qualified graduates possessing a undergraduate degree in ITDS. The graduate with a high GPA, Cooperative Education job experience and active in one or more extracurricular student organizations can expect to be actively recruited by major national and international firms. The career prospects for information systems (IS) professionals look quite favourable.

The following job descriptions are provided to help you understand the kinds of opportunities available. Job titles may vary among organizations.

- *Junior Systems Analyst (Consultant):* Work with users in defining business problems/needs; provide systems specifications and systems design for user. The analyst is a part of a project team.
- *Junior Application Programmer:* Responsible for writing and/or maintaining computer programmes for business applications. May also be responsible for the development and design of computer programmes.
- *Junior Systems Analyst / Programmer:* Performs the job of both the systems analyst and the applications programmer.

- *Computer Marketing Representative:* Sells computer mainframes, mini/micro systems, special purpose systems, peripherals and supplies and/or services.

After one or more years in an entry-level position, one can move up the career ladder. An individual's career choice, motivation and success in an initial assignment are important factors for moving into new positions, as well as size of company. Positions such as these many be available:

- ***Vice President of MIS (CIO):*** The senior executive for all corporate information systems assets. Responsible for long range planning, budgeting and operations.
- ***Director of Information Services:*** In charge of information systems assets at the divisional/departmental level. Responsibilities parallel those of corporate officers, but may be at least partially guided by decisions made at the corporate level.
- ***Director of Communications:*** Responsible for planning, implementing and managing all corporate telecommunication facilities: includes voice, data, video, graphics and other content.
- ***Services Coordinator/User Liaison:*** Interfaces between IS department and users; represents users when operational problems occur.
- ***Systems Analysts:*** Confers with users to define and formulate logical statements of business problems and devise procedures for solutions through use of information systems.
- ***Applications Programmer:*** Develops, designs, prepares and tests computer programmes.
- ***Systems Analyst/Programmer:*** Performs the functions of both the systems analysis and applications programming positions.
- ***Operating Systems Programmer:*** Programmes, maintains and introduces modifications to systems software. Usually requires background in computer science.

- ***Data Administrator:*** Plans, organizes and manages organization's datasets. Establishes standards, maintains directory, coordinates corporate database needs.
- ***Database Administrator:*** Analyzes an application's computerized information requirements, coordinates data collection and storage needs.
- ***Data Communications/Telecommunications Manager:*** Responsible for the design of data communications networks and the installation and operation of data links.
- ***Data Communications Analyst:*** Specializes in network design, traffic analysis and data communications software.
- ***Manager of Computer Operations:*** In charge of computer operations, including scheduling, assignment of operators and monitoring efficiency.
- ***Production Control Supervisor:*** Responsible for setting up and scheduling jobs for processing so as to maximize quality, utilization and turnaround requirements.
- ***Data Entry Supervisor:*** Responsible for a staff that performs data entry and verification functions.
- ***Director of User Support:*** Coordinates and manages all user support services; includes help desk, training and technical support.
- ***User Services Staff (Help Desk — First Line Support):*** Knowledgeable in broad aspects of first line support; provides guidance to users, helps in debugging specific problems and understanding system procedures.
- ***Technical Support (Help Desk—Second Line Support):*** Supports and does problem determination in specific technical areas such as networks, servers, databases, hardware, etc.
- ***Technical Writer:*** Writes manuals for application systems for user and internal reference. Requires sound knowledge of technical English, as well as information technology.
- ***Remote Site Administrator:*** In a distributed environment, manages a remote site as sole or additional

duty. Responsible for physical security, sets operations priorities, supervises operations and initiates problem-determination actions as required.

- ***Training and Education Specialist:*** Organizes, prepares and conducts training courses for IS and user personnel.
- ***Computer Security Specialist:*** Concerned with the protection of data and computer resources, including networks.
- ***EDP Auditors (Accounting Oriented):*** Perform detailed evaluations of systems and operational procedures. Insure systems and procedural integrity and accuracy.
- ***Field Service Engineer:*** Vendor-trained electronic technician who can service mechanical equipment, replacing and repairing malfunctioning electronic components; also performs software-problem determination. Requires additional training in computer electronics.

Job Levels (an example)

- ***Manager:*** Advanced degree and minimum five years' experience or equivalent combination. Strong management and communications skills, works independently, performs personnel evaluation, budgeting, progress reporting and project management.
- ***Lead:*** BS and minimum four years experience in IS with two of those years in a supervisory capacity. Works on own and performs all levels of supervision, generally as a project leader.
- ***Senior:*** BS and minimum four years experience including some supervision.
- ***Intermediate:*** BS and minimum two years experience or equivalent combination. Works on own most of the time, requiring direction on some activities.
- ***Junior:*** Two to four years college and minimum six months experience or equivalent combination. Directly supervised but works on own on some aspects of job.

Position: Information Technology Specialist 5—Desktop Application Support.

Division: Information Services, Computing, Network & Support Services

Location: Tumwater

Recruitment: 07.125

Salary: $4,315 – 5,522 Month, Range 62

Opens: April 19, 2007

Closes: May 4, 2007 at 5:00 p.m.

Principal Responsibilities: This position is the expert level technician providing configuration and integration for the agency's standard software running in the desktop environment. It ensures consistent and quality implementation and complex technical support of software supporting the agency's ability to provide timely services to its customers.

The Information Technology Specialist 5-Desktop Application Support will be accountable in the following respects:

- Responsible for providing expert level support and documentation to agency staff with application services, such as design or configuration and integration of applications for desktop PC's, notebooks and tablet PC's.
- Provide support in desktop hardware, software, Windows operating systems, integration methodology (software and hardware), application integration documentation and connectivity documentation; utilize good working knowledge of network environment including hardware (LAN, WAN, switches and routers) and software (Active Directory, global catalogue, domain controllers, print and file services, DNS and WINS) as part of everyday work.
- Coordinate vendor support as needed to ensure desktop application and operating system stability. Technical analysis for this position includes problem isolation, problem identification and problem-solving that impact agency business; provide support to agency security patching, manage firewall updates and SMS rollouts.

- Provide specialized and ongoing technical support to maintain desktop applications performance and availability, such as making operating system upgrades, monitoring performance logs, deploying applications via automated methods and reviewing and updating application configuration settings.
- Provide leadership, expert consultation and project management skills for assigned projects ensuring appropriate documentation, communication and timely completion.

Qualifications of the successful candidate include: 3-5 years experience supporting a Microsoft Windows desktop system comprised of 500+ customers in multiple locations in a multi-tier network environment (*i.e.* includes desktop, server, LAN/WAN, centralized web services and mainframe services.

Knowledge of: Application integration processes; packaging software tool such as Wise Packaging Studio for integration; software installation scripts and/or MSI configuration; network and desktop computing environments including hardware configuration with experience in software distribution tools such as SMS.

Skills and Abilities:

- Strong understanding and/or experience with project management.
- Excellent documentation skills to create detailed reports of application integration performed.
- Ability to edit existing integration documentation to show all modifications as a part of all work assignments.
- Communicate well in writing.
- Must understand the importance of teamwork on projects.
- Ability to pro-actively identify, analyze and resolve business technical problems.
- Ability to lift computer equipment weighing up to 50 pounds.
- Ability to travel by car and overnight, occasionally, to remote field office locations.
- Must possess a valid Washington State Drivers License.

Application Process: We are looking for evidence that you have the skills and abilities required for this job. The information you provide will be used as a basis for deciding who will be selected for the next step in the process.

Special Note: Prior to any new appointment into L&I, a background check, including criminal record history, will be conducted.

1. Fill out the L&I Employment Application.
2. Include a Letter of Interest describing how you meet the qualification, skills and abilities for this position.
3. All applicants must submit answers to the following (3) supplemental questions in one page or less:

Career Opportunities

The Miller School of Medicine presents a challenging and rewarding work environment for information technology professionals. Technology teams here provide services and administer systems that are nationally recognized for their innovation and leading-edge vision.

We welcome you to search the Careers web site and apply to any positions that you feel match your skills and experience.

You can search for "Information Technology" within the "Job Category" field to see listings for our department at the Medical Center. Select "Search All" in the Department field to include listings with the Medical Center Information Technology department as well as other medical campus departments with IT positions.

Information Systems Manager

Organizations have demanded greater use of newer technologies in recent years to stay competitive. Important issues involving the use of electronic or online commerce include when and how a company incorporates these new technologies. Information and Computer systems managers are essential in planning an organization's future, maintaining Internet support and supervising security operations.

Managers are in charge of all planning and developing phases of a firm's activities. They consult with executive managers about plans and goals for the future while working with teams in the conceptual capacity and developmental process of particular products.

Computer and information systems managers supervise the programming, support and analyst departments of an organization. They work in the planning and developing process of all implemental phases of computer activities. This includes installing software and hardware, design programming, networking and Internet maintenance. More managers are even involved in network security areas, in addition to strategically evaluating organizational needs relating to equipment and information. They set tasks and delegate responsibilities for workers and are essentially on top of the latest updates in technology news and advancement to help the organization stay competitive.

Management information systems (MIS) directors oversee all resources and systems within a firm. They are often subordinate to a head information officer and supervise the work of other subordinate information workers. They manage the many services available to employees, including the help desk and making valuable suggestions to technological practice as it relates to software and hardware development. These managers are essential to an organization in ensuring the fluidity, efficiency, availability and security of all services.

Project Managers work out the firm's necessary scheduling and budget requirements for specific projects. They work in all phases of the project with all of the key players in the process, including clients, technological specialists, consultants and sales representatives. Security enhancement is becoming a more common type of project for these managers.

LAN/WAN (Local Area Network/Wide Area Network) managers work in the administration and design process of a local firm's internal network. They essentially manage and the operation of the network and all of it's elemental features—including, applications and systems software, hardware and others.

Strong interpersonal skills will help computer and information specialists work with and coordinate activities of different workers. They coordinate activities with top management executives, departmental managers, equipment suppliers and all other contractors.

Information Systems Manager Career Training and Job Qualifications: Computer and Information systems managers must be capable of working with subordinates in technical areas while helping top management and customers understand in simple terms. Thus, managers are best to have had prior formal working and education experience.

It is common for computer and information systems managers to have prior experience in one or more of several specialty areas, including information technology, systems analysis and programming. While a bachelor's degree will usually qualify one for a management job, having a Master's degree that emphasizes both technology and business administration is highly favourable for employers. This is such as business and technology is becoming interdependent in business decision-making. Information technology degrees are sometimes offered in management-information, which combines communication and business skills with core information technology. Sometimes, if a manager has adequate training and experience all that is needed is an associate's degree. A manager in this situation will often go on to earn a Master's degree at some point in order to further their advancement.

A wide amount of skills in technology and business will aid computer and information systems managers. Employers look favorably upon potential managers with backgrounds in both software and other specific technology and business. The importance of manager's decisions that affect the business has only been augmented by the growth in e-commerce. Managers should have the ability to work with all people, including customers, in this process.

Managers will benefit from having strong leadership and communication skills in their dealings with people within and without the organization. This is especially important in the collaboration process within a project team. In general, computer and information systems managers exercise an important role in representing a firm when interacting with outside individuals.

Job and Employment Opportunities for Information Systems Managers: Over the next decade, computer and information systems manager occupations are likely to expand at a rate faster than most other occupations. This is especially so as technology evolves and requires more workers and managers to guide this process. Moreover, employee and manager turnovers will bring added job opportunities. Those with a Master's degree in business technology and management and those with good interpersonal skills will be most qualified for these opportunities.

Notwithstanding the economic recession, the future holds strong for computer and information systems managers. Organizations will be implementing complex networks in order to stay competitive in this field. Thus, more managers are required to maintain these networks in smooth operation.

Es electronic commerce continues to rise, so will the need for network security. This has become an increasingly vital issue in recent times, as organizations are required to understand potential attacks and vulnerabilities, such as those caused by viruses and hackers. Managers will continue to be needed to maintain such things as "cybersecurity" and assume roles of leadership in order to sustain the integrity of the computing departments. As a result, demand for managers with strong security knowledge will grow rapidly in the future.

The roles that computer and information systems managers fill will continue to change with the evolution of e-commerce and customer inter-relationships. Additionally, wireless Internet technology will result in the rising demand for managers with both technical and business knowledge.

Historical Earnings Information: Depending on specialty are skills area, approximate annual salaries for computer and information systems managers range from $47,000 for the bottom ten percent to $140,000 for the top ten percent. In 2002, average annual earnings for these positions were $85,000. Different specialties include computer systems design and services, company management, insurance providers, credit intermediation and work involved with Universities or technical schools.

Robert Half International found in 2003 that approximate average earnings ranged from around $82,000 to $151,000 for upper-level information technology managers. The National Association of Colleges and Employees surveyed and found that averages for entry-level positions were around $55,000 for those with a Master's degree in Business Administration, an undergraduate degree and less than one year experience. Additionally, entry-level salaries for individuals with a graduate degree in data processing or management information systems averaged around $44,000.

An added incentive to becoming an upper-level manager is the many associated benefits that others do not qualify for. These include stock option plans, bonuses and expense accounts.

Computer Software Engineering

The world has felt a the explosive impact of computers and the IT industry in its very core and the increasing need for computers in the daily life of people has made it imperative that new designs and new computer software systems be developed so that advancing technology can be applied in a growing range of applications. The work assigned to people who are called computer software engineers evolves very fast, which reflects the changes in technology as well as the increase of new specializations which keep cropping up in this field along with the preferences and practices of employers. The principles and knowledge of computer science, engineering and mathematical analysis are employed by computer software engineers for designing, developing, testing and evaluating the software and the systems that computers use to carry out various applications.

Software engineers who work in applications or systems development are engaged in analyzing user needs and designing, constructing, testing and maintaining computer applications software or systems. Various kinds of software like software for operating systems and network distribution and compilers, which convert programmes for execution on a computer, are developed by a software engineer. In the programming or coding fields, software engineers give instructions to a computer, line by line; on how on perform a function or operation. These engineers are also geared to tackle technical problems and hitches. Although these engineers need to possess string programming skills, they are more occupied with the development of algorithms and in analyzing and solving problems in programming than with writing codes.

Computer Applications Software Engineers: Computer applications software engineers are engaged in analyzing user needs as well as designing, constructing and maintaining computer applications software and specialized utility programmes. Various programming languages are used by these engineers, which are chosen regarding the required purpose for which a computer programme would be used. C and C++ are the programming languages that are most commonly while Java, with Fortran and COBOL are used less extensively. Either packaged systems and software systems or specific customized applications are designed and developed by software engineers.

Computer Systems Software Engineers: Computer systems software engineers are involved in coordinating the construction of the computer systems of an organization, maintaining them and planning their future growth. They work with a particular company and coordinate the needs and demands of the computer needs of every department by ordering, inventory, billing and payroll recordkeeping. Suggestions are also made about a computer systems' technical direction. A company's intranet (the network which links computers inside a organization and ease communication among the various departments) is also constructed by these engineers.

Systems software engineers work for companies that need configuration, implementation and installation of complete computer systems. These engineers may also be part of the marketing or sales staff and serve as the chief technical resource for these sales officers, staff, as well as customers. They may even engage in product sales and provide continued technical support to the buyers and consumers.

Computer software engineers are usually a part of the team that designs and develops advanced hardware, software and systems. Thus, until a finished product is developed and released, workers from various branches including those of engineering, marketing, production and design collaborate with each other, of which computer engineers are a basic part.

In 2002, computer software engineers had around 675,000 jobs. Around 394,000 were computer applications software engineers while about 281,000 were computer systems software engineers. Though these engineers are employed in every industry, the largest concentration of computer software engineers (about 30 percent) is in computer systems design and related services. A large number of computer software engineers are also hired by other industries that include government agencies, producers of computers and related electronic equipment, as well as colleges and universities.

The employers of computer software engineers cover start-up companies to established industry leaders and thus include a large number of clientele. As the use of the Internet, e-mail and other communications systems increases, firms from electronics to engineering which were traditionally associated as unrelated disciplines will expand, hiring more and more such engineers.

Engineering firms specializing in building bridges and power plants, for example, also hire computer software engineers for designing and developing advanced geographic data systems and automated drafting systems. Communications industries also require computer software engineers, with whose help the personal communications market could be tapped into. The major communications companies have many job opportunities for both computer software applications and computer systems engineers.

A growing number of computer software engineers are also employed on a temporary or contract basis (with many being self-employed) who work on their own as consultants. Some of these consultants work for firms that specialize in the development and maintenance of the client companies' Web sites and intranets. Consulting opportunities for software engineers are expected to increase because businesses need help to manage, upgrade and customize increasingly complex computer systems. In 2002, around 21,000 computer software engineers were self-employed.

Software Engineering Career Training & Job Qualifications: Most employers have a preference for candidates who have at least a bachelor's degree, a broad knowledge and experience with a variety of computer systems and technologies. The common degree concentrations for applications software engineers are computer science or software engineering; for systems software engineers it is computer science or computer information systems. A Graduate degree is preferred for some of the more complex work.

The academic programmes in software engineering emphasize software and might be offered either as a degree option or in conjunction with computer science degrees. The increase of emphasis on computer security proves that software engineers with advanced degrees, including mathematics and systems design, will be sought after by software developers, government agencies and consulting firms which specialize in information assurance and security. Candidates who seek software engineering jobs will enhance their employment opportunities by participation in internship or co-op programmes which are offered through their schools.

These experiences will provide the students with both theoretical knowledge and experience, making them more attractive candidates for employers though inexperienced college graduates will usually be hired by large computer and consulting firms which train new hires in intensive, company-based programmes. Many firms mentor the new employees are mentored and the mentors usually have an input into the new hires' evaluations.

For systems software engineering jobs which need professionals who have a college degree, a bachelor's degree in computer science or computer information systems is common. For systems engineering jobs which place less emphasis on employees having a computer-related degree, computer training programme which lead to a certification are offered by systems software vendors, including Microsoft, Novell and Oracle. These programmes usually extend from 1 to 4 weeks, but the worker is not required to attend the classes in order to sit for a certification exam; many study guides and materials are also available which help students prepare for the exams. However, many training authorities are of the view that programme certification alone is not sufficient for most software engineering jobs.

That is the reason that professional certification is now being offered by the Institute of Electrical and Electronics Engineers (IEEE) Computer Society. In order for a candidate to be classified as a Certified Software Development Professional, he needs a bachelor's degree as well as work experience which shows a person's mastery of a relevant body of knowledge and they must pass a written exam.

The people who are interested in jobs as computer software engineers require strong problem-solving and analytical skills. They must also have good communication skills so that they can efficiently interact with team members, other staff and the customers they meet. Also, a good deal of concentration as well as an eye for detail is required of these candidates because they often deal with a number of tasks simultaneously.

Like in most occupations, the opportunities for promotions for computer software engineers directly relate to experience. The entry-level computer software engineers are likely to test and verify ongoing designs and as they gain more experience, they may be involved in designing and developing software. Eventually, these engineers may advance to become project managers, managers of information systems, or chief information officers. Some computer software engineers with an experience and expertise of several years may be offered lucrative opportunities to work as systems designers or independent consultants or may start their own computer consultation firms.

These days, because of the rapid technological advances in the computer field, employers always demand new skills. Thus computer software engineers must continually strive to keep abreast of the changes in this dynamic field and upgrade the level of their knowledge and skill. In order to help them keep up-to-date with the advancing technology, continuing education and professional development seminars are offered by employers and software vendors, colleges and universities, private training institutions and professional computing societies.

Computer Software Engineering Job and Employment Opportunities: Computer software engineers are projected to be one of the fastest growing occupations from 2002 to 2012. Rapid employment growth in the computer systems design and related services industry, which employs the greatest number of computer software engineers, should result in highly favourable opportunities for those college graduates with at least a bachelor's degree in computer engineering or computer science and practical experience working with computers. Employers will continue to seek computer professionals with strong programming, systems analysis, interpersonal and business skills.

Despite the recent downturn in information technology, employment of computer software engineers is expected to increase much faster than the average for all occupations, as businesses and other organizations adopt and integrate new technologies and seek to maximize the efficiency of their computer systems. Job growth will not be as rapid as during the previous decade however, as the software industry begins to mature and as routine software engineering work is increasingly outsourced overseas. Competition among businesses will continue to create an incentive for increasingly sophisticated technological innovations and organizations will need more computer software engineers to implement these changes. In addition to jobs created through employment growth, many job openings will result annually from the need to replace workers who move into managerial positions, transfer to other occupations, or leave the labour force.

Demand for computer software engineers will increase as computer networking continues to grow. For example, the expanding integration of Internet technologies and the explosive growth in electronic commerce—doing business on the Internet—have resulted in rising demand for computer software engineers who can develop Internet, intranet and World Wide

Web applications. Likewise, expanding electronic data-processing systems in business, telecommunications, government and other settings continue to become more sophisticated and complex. Growing numbers of systems software engineers will be needed to implement, safeguard and update systems and resolve problems. Consulting opportunities for computer software engineers also should continue to grow as businesses seek help to manage, upgrade and customize their increasingly complex computer systems.

New growth areas will continue to arise from rapidly evolving technologies. The increasing uses of the Internet, the proliferation of Web sites and "mobile" technology such as the wireless Internet have created a demand for a wide variety of new products. As individuals and businesses rely more on hand-held computers and wireless networks, it will be necessary to integrate current computer systems with this new, more mobile technology. Also, information security concerns have given rise to new software needs. Concerns over "cybersecurity" should result in businesses and government continuing to invest heavily in security software that protects their networks and vital electronic infrastructure from attack. The expansion of this technology in the next 10 years will lead to an increased need for computer engineers to design and develop the software and systems to run these new applications and that will allow them to be integrated into older systems.

As with other information technology jobs, employment growth of computer software engineers may be tempered somewhat by an increase in contracting out of software development abroad. Firms may look to cut costs by shifting operations to foreign countries with highly educated workers who have strong technical skills.

Historical Earnings Information: In 2002, the median salaries received by computer applications software engineers annually, who hired as full time workers were around $70,900. The middle 50 percent received salaries that lay between $55,510 and $88,660. The lowest 10 percent earned below $44,830, while the highest 10 percent received above $109,800. In 2002, the median salaries paid by the industries that hired the largest numbers of computer applications software engineers on an annual basis were:

- Software publishers—$76,450
- Navigational, measuring, electro-medical and control instruments manufacturing—$75,890
- Computer systems design and related services—$71,890
- Architectural, engineering and related services—$70,090
- Management of companies and enterprises—$67,260

In 2002, the median salaries received by computer systems software engineers annually, who were hired on a full time basis, were around $74,040. The middle 50 percent received salaries that lay between $58,500 and $91,160. The lowest 10 percent received waged which were below $45,890, while the highest 10 percent received wages above 111,600. In 2002, the industries which hired the largest numbers of computer systems software engineers paid median annual salaries like shown below:

- Scientific research and development services—$82,270
- Software publishers—$77,120
- Navigational, measuring, electro-medical and control instruments manufacturing—$76,200
- Computer systems design and related services—$73,460
- Wired telecommunications carriers—$68,510

In a 2003, salary survey conducted by the National Association of Colleges and Employers, computer engineers with a bachelor's degree were offered starting wages of $51,343 on an average and those with a master's degree earned around $64,200. Graduate students with a bachelor's degree in computer science received $47,109 as salaries on an average.

In a Robert Half International salary survey in 2003, software engineers in software development received starting offers that lay between $64,250 to $97,000.

Apart from the usual benefits and job perks, computer software engineers may also be given the option of sharing company profits and stock and be provided with a company car with a mileage allowance.

Statistician Careers, Jobs and Education Information: Career and Job Highlights for Statisticians:

- Having earned a degree in statistics does not necessarily lead to jobs with statistician profiles
- Most statistician jobs require no fewer qualifications a master's degree in mathematics of statistics.
- Opportunities are likely to continue to exist for people with statistician degrees, despite the decline in growth expectations

Statistician Career: Statistics essentially involves putting mathematics to scientific use in the form of data comparison, analysis and presentation. Statisticians use this knowledge to design, collect and interpret data experiments surrounding many different fields of industry. This includes fields of economics, medicine, psychology, marketing, public health, biology, sports and others. Even military considerations take statistical procedures for approval of certain strategies and sanctions.

Statisticians use sampling techniques to determine sizes of relative populations and demographics. This process is achieved by surveying portions of large groups. They determine the size of group samples and the methods for carrying these samples out. This includes stylizing the instructions and questions to be used in surveys. Finally, statisticians summarize, analyze and interpret the resultant data.

Statisticians are also heavily involved in the development of products and quality factors. They often work for automobile, pharmaceutical, or computer software companies in trial testing and product evaluation. Apart from development, statisticians are also involved with the manufacturing, asset, liability and risk management and marketing departments of firms.

Most government organizations and agencies hire statisticians to evaluate population, demographic and economic measurements. Many other environmental, scientific and agricultural agencies hire statisticians for similar type of work in their respective fields. Even national defense organizations hire statisticians to assess weapons and strategy effectiveness.

Different job titles exist for different statistical specializations. Biostatisticians and epidemiologists are two examples of job titles within the health industry. Econometricians work in areas involving economic research and data.

Statistician Career Training and Job Qualifications: Most statistical jobs require at least a master's degree in mathematics or statistics. More advanced academic research in statistics require at least a higher-level institution requires a master's degree and Ph.D. in the same field. Entry-level jobs in other areas of research, such as industrial, require many experienced years of work and study.

Qualification for statistician jobs in the Federal Government requires a bachelor's degree with certain accredited hours in statistics and mathematics. To be a mathematical statistician in the Government requires a total of twenty-four hours in combined statistics and mathematics, with particular concern for differential equations, vector analysis and calculus. Numerous schools have degrees and necessary course available in these areas of research. Statistical majors usually require courses in probability theory, calculus and statistical methods and modelling. This is in addition to the algebra, mathematical design and analysis courses usually incorporated in the undergraduate programme.

Around 140 schools of higher learning offer master's degrees in statistics, while around 90 offer doctoral degrees. Numerous schools have upper-level and graduate level statistic courses in economics, engineering, business, education and psychology. Although undergraduate training is not required for acceptance, graduate programmes prefer students to have had prior mathematical training.

Statistics are used widely in computer programmes and thus computer science training is also beneficial. For jobs involving product quality management, training physical science and engineering may be required. Any area of health science training is helpful to move into pharmaceutical jobs and business or economics education is good for business analysis, forecasting and market research.

Having strong interpersonal skills will also help statisticians in communicating technical concerns to people unfamiliar with specific programmes. For those working in the private sector, a general knowledge of business and economics is highly beneficial. Entry-level statisticians work under supervision but are soon likely to advance on to greater responsibility jobs. These promotions or advancements are greatest for those with graduate degrees in the respective fields.

Job and Employment Opportunities for Statisticians: Over the course of the next decade, job growth is likely to decline. Many opportunities should nonetheless be open to job seekers with the appropriate degree. Instead of having a typical statistician job profile, however, these workers may instead work in analysis areas for science, computer and business fields. Although job growth is not likely to expand, opportunities are still afforded through employee turnovers and career transfers.

The most qualified candidates for jobs are those with a graduate education in statistics relating to finance, engineering, computer science and biology. The National government has many openings for statisticians within its different departments and these jobs are considered to be highly competitive due to their lower expectation requirements for beginner jobs. Those certified with the State are usually able to find high school teaching positions.

Statisticians work for manufacturing firms in areas such as aircraft, motor vehicles, pharmaceuticals, food and chemicals. A pharmaceutical firm may employ a statistician to evaluate drug efficiency. A motor vehicle company may hire statistician for quality control purposes in testing automobiles. They may also work with scientists and engineers in researching and analyzing new product development. Many software firms also hire statisticians for quality control and software development.

Businesses work with statisticians in evaluating overall business-run efficiency and profit. Statisticians in this field also offer consulting services to another business. Generally, statisticians ought to have current computer skills and awareness, including programming and software equipment.

Historical Earnings Information: Approximate annual salaries for statisticians range from $30,000 for the bottom ten percent to $92,000 for the top ten percent. Average earnings in 2002 were around $57,000.

Computer Science, Technology and Database Administration

Careers and Jobs: Computer Science and Technology Careers and Job Highlights:

- General job pre-requisites are a two-year computer science degree upwards to a graduate degree.
- Technological advancements are likely to boost employment opportunities with more rapid rates than ever before
- Many job opportunities presently exist

Computer Science, Technology and Database Administration Career: A rising demand for skilled employees to develop new software and hardware technologies has resulted from the expansion of computer use. New and specialized job opportunities—including database administrators, computer scientists and analysts—will increasingly rise out of evolving technologies and employer practices.

Systems analysts work with the individual needs of organizations by helping them solve their computer and technology problems. In this way, the organization is able to maintain optimal efficiency in investment, business and personnel procedures. Computer scientists devise new ways of developing existing and up-and-coming computer systems. This includes designing new hardware and software systems to maximize a computer's power. Systems analysts generally work within a specified field related determined by the organization they work for. Accounting, business, scientific and engineering systems are but a few of these fields. Systems analysts job titles are often the same as systems architects / developers.

First, analysts determine the problems with the system through discussion with the managers. Goals and solutions are then determined and implemented, using methods such as information engineering, mathematical and data modelling and cost accounting. Determining the proper inputs and outputs of the system serve to meet the individual users' needs. To assist the management in deciding financial capacity in implementing these new systems, analysts often prepare cost-benefit and return analyses.

After the system is accepted, analysts run tests and observations to determine what hardware and software is needed to set it up. To eliminate the possibility of any future errors in the system analysts will make specification charts and diagrams for programmers to work with. Analysts with heavier experience are often called software quality assurance analysts. This type of analyst performs all of the normal work in addition to finding problems and solutions to computer systems.

Programmer-analysts must be proficient in both programming and systems analysis in order to design and improve computer software. As this becomes process becomes more mainstream, more of these analysts will work with client server applications development, multimedia and Internet technology and object-oriented programming languages.

The need for different computer systems to communicate with each other poises one problem for expanding computer use. Systems analysts try to make computer systems compatible within an organization for reasons of keeping information accounting records current, as well as maintaining budget projections and sales figures. "Networking" is a common procedure used by analysts to connect computers both internally (in offices or departments) and externally (internet and e-mail). The main objective is to make information accessible from a mainframe computer or server. Thus, analysts have to be able to design the right hardware and software to allow this access.

Network systems and data communications analysts design and evaluate different types of systems. These systems include wide area networks (WAN), local area networks (LAN), Internet and Intranet's and others. In addition to researching for the necessary products and hardware and software components, analysts do network analysis, modelling and planning. Telecommunications specialists work with the overlap of computer and communications development. Many design and development occupations have grown out of the rising use of the World Wide Web and computer graphics. Jobs such as webmasters maintain all performance and technical aspects of a website. This includes approving of site content and speed access. Web designers usually maintain day-to-date site design. Many new jobs have been created as a result of emerging web-technologies. Webmasters maintain the performance of a website, while Internet developers create and design websites.

Computer scientists work in the diverse areas of researching, inventing, or theorizing. Their jobs are categorized by the amount of expertise they have in a particular field. Academic institutions will usually have computer scientists work with hardware, language design and complexity theory. Others develop the use of human-computer interaction, robotics, or virtual reality. Computer scientists in the private sector also work with information technologies, designing language and other programming tools, knowledge-based systems, theory application and computer games.

There is an increasing demand for organizations to be able to store, manage and extract data more efficiently as electronic business is creating larger amounts of data every day. Database administrators work with database management systems to ensure performance, understand the database specifications and add new users. Deciphering the necessary requirements and changes does this. These administrators usually plan security and backup systems to ensure the safe keeping of the rapidly growing amount of data that exists.

In 2002, nearly 100,000 jobs were distributed among computer and information-scientists, systems and data analysts and database administrators. The majority of computer science occupations exist in systems design and service industries. Commercial services include facilities and data-processing management, software installation, integration design and programming. Service organizations, ISPs and web search portals often hire analysts, scientists and administrators.

Governments and financial and educational institutions also have heavy concentrations of computer workers.

Many computer programmers work independently as contractors or consultants for companies needing specialized knowledge in areas of computer languages and application. An organization may contract with an independent analyst or an agency to install a computer or software system. Hiring programmers through contractual agreements rather than as permanent employees is an efficient way of harnessing people with the specific skills needed without having to train or retrain newcomers. Contractual agreements range from a few weeks to more than a year.

Computer Science, Technology and Database Administration Training and Qualifications: Employers recognize the requirements for high skill and education levels as technology continues to change. People with both technical and communication skills are now important as companies seek to hire employees that can handle various responsibilities. Most companies prefer that you have formal college experience, whether it is a bachelor's degree or, for placement into more complex jobs, graduate school experience. In some cases all that is needed is a two-year degree or some related experience.

A bachelor's degree in information science, computer science, or management information systems (MIS) is required of systems and programmer-analysts, as well as database administrator positions for a good job in related fields. Most business schools have an MIS programme as these programmes emphasize management and business computing. As businesses become more internet-oriented, a master's degree in business administration (MBA) with an emphasis in information systems is becoming more desirable of employers. An associate's degree or certificate usually is adequate training for placement as a network or data communication analysts, such as a web-master. A doctorate degree is usually necessary to do the complex work of computer and information science.

It is possible for anyone with a degree to find a job in a computer field despite employer preference for specialized computer science degrees. It all depends on employer's needs, especially as it relates to technological change. Given the demand for Internet skills, workers with the ability to develop cutting edge technology are highly competitive. Also, deadlines for projects can influence an employer's decision.

Many associate degrees offered by community colleges and independent technical institutes are more occupation-oriented than most four-year degree programmes. The more focused type of training is more beneficial to certain job areas. Good interpersonal, problem-solving and analytical skills are important for employers seeking individuals with computer experience and knowledge. A good form of preparation for job seekers is to enrol in computer science or systems courses. For business oriented systems analysis, employers generally require some form of management experience. Knowledge of physical sciences, engineering, or applied mathematics is important for jobs in the scientific environment. Finally, for webmasters or developers, experience with graphic design is essential.

Internships and co-op programmes offer job seekers with ample opportunities to boost their qualifications for jobs. For those who transfer between computer-oriented industries, experience in the relevant industry is very important, whether it be accounting, banking, or financial services. Some have enrolled in courses to increase their knowledge in these and other fields. A computer programmer, to illustrate, might transfer to be a systems analyst. Additionally, A financial analyst with knowledge of computer systems might transfer to be a computer support specialist in a related field. Strong reasoning, problem solving and interpersonal skills are required of systems analysts, database administrators and computer scientists who must be able to deal in detail with several tasks at once. Most specialists work in groups and thus must be able to work well with others involved, including programmers, computer personnel and managers.

Computer scientists employed in academic institutions and other private practices can move upwards to leadership or administrative positions as perhaps the head of a department, lead systems analyst, project manager or chief information officer. To become a chief technology officer depends on ones experience with managing data and ensuring its security. Specialists with emphasis in a particular field may find it advantageous to become independent consultants or start their own business.

Continuing ones studies in the computer field is essential to stay up-to-date with emerging technologies. Many continuing education opportunities are available through colleges and universities and other training institutions, including employers and professional seminars.

To achieve qualifications and work-ability in a particular field, one may seek technical or professional certification. Many product and software companies offer certification to professionals. Certification is essentially a standard process in the industry. To become certified as a database management, for example, is one standard step on the path to becoming a database administrator. Voluntary and professional certification, both offered by product vendors and software firms, has the ability to make a job seeker more competitive.

Registered Apprenticeship

The Registered Apprenticeship model is well known and has served the training needs of a variety of businesses and industries over time. The basic components of the model are especially suited to the information technology industry.

The apprenticeship model helps participants attain high performance through a cohesive process which links formal instruction in the form of a degree or certification with a standardized process of delivering and measuring hands-on/ on-the-job learning (OJL).

For decades, registered apprenticeship programmes have been successful by combining on-the-job learning with classroom theory supported by a strong mentoring component. The apprentice goes through a structured programme established by the employer that includes incremental wage increases until he or she completes the course of training.

How it Works in Information Technology?: Apprenticeship programmes are designed to respond to real-world business goals, such as increased productivity/performance, greater efficiency and improved customer retention. Employers in the Information Technology industry often partner with credentialing and licensing agencies to ensure that apprentices get the training and instruction needed to meet applicable requirements.

A key organization involved in IT competency attainment, certification and apprenticeship is the Computer Technology Industry Association (CompTIA), which has partnered with organizations such as IBM, McDonald's and more recently DeVry University.

Some apprenticeable information technology occupations are:

- Computer Operator
- Computer Programmer
- Graphic Designer
- Internet working Technician
- IT Project Manager

Database Administrator

Database administrators manage and supervise computer databases. They make sure the database is accurate, secure and up-to-date. Database administrators work on ways to reorganise or restructure databases to make them easier to use. They set up backup systems in case the database breaks down.

Work Activities: Database administrators are responsible for organisations' computer databases. A growing number of organisations use databases to keep and update large amounts of information, for example, customers' details.

Retail companies use databases to find out more about their customers, for example, their spending patterns, in order to make informed decisions about new products and marketing strategies. Supermarkets collect information about their customers through their use of loyalty cards. A charity may use a database to keep a record of its supporters; the charity may then contact those supporters by mailshot when it launches a new fundraising campaign. The police and the health service have large and complex databases.

Database administrators make sure the database is accurate, secure and used effectively. A strict data protection law governs the use and security of information held on databases. It is up to the database administrator to make sure that only authorised people can look at what can be very personal details, for example, medical information. Also, people have a right to access database information about themselves; administrators may have to negotiate this access.

Administrators work closely with people who use the database, finding out whether there are any problems and assessing the system's capacity to cope with demand. They support users, for example, showing them how to search the database for specific information.

They may also modify the database to make it easier to use or to expand it, perhaps by adding new spaces or 'fields' to hold additional data. They reorganise and restructure the data to better suit users' needs.

Problem solving plays a big part in this job; administrators must set up reliable backup systems in case data is lost or a breakdown occurs. They are also closely involved in deciding how to design and plan databases.

Some organisations use alternative job titles such as information centre manager, database administration manager or database controller.

Database administrators may work closely with analysts on database design.

Personal Qualities and Skills: To be a database administrator, you must have good technical knowledge of databases.

You must also have strong communication skills, to explain how the database works to its users.

You will need strong organisational skills; you may be responsible for several databases, making sure that all of them are up-to-date and accurate.

Knowledge of data protection issues and access rights is very important. You must be willing to keep up-to-date with any changes in data protection laws and make sure you apply legislation throughout the organisation you work for.

Pay and Opportunities: The pay rates given below are approximate. Salaries are in the range of £16,500—£21,000 a year, rising to £27,500—£35,500. Higher earners can make around £45,000 a year. Salaries may include performance related pay, profit sharing or company bonuses.

Database administrators work 35 hours from Monday to Friday, but may work some late evenings when deadlines require, or work out of hours if systems fail.

Employment is in every sector of industry and commerce, especially with banks, building societies, insurance companies and others in the finance sector and in public service (local and central government departments). This is a fast-growing area of employment.

The following information is sourced from government statistics. The government's definition of types of job is slightly different to that used in this programme. For this type of job, the most relevant Government-defined occupation is 'IT operations technicians'.

In 2001 there were 7,500 people working as IT operations technicians in Scotland. 35 in every 10,000 employees working in Scotland were employed as IT operations technicians.

Estimates of projected future job openings requiring new entrants to the jobs market are available, but not at the level of detail of 'IT operations technicians'. It is estimated that over the five years between 2003 and 2008 there will be a need for 6000 new employees to fill vacancies in the broader occupational type of 'IT Service Delivery Occupations'. 2 out of every 20 employees work part time in this type of job.

Entry Routes and Training: Database administrators are usually experienced systems designers or programmers. Many employers ask for a degree or Higher National Diploma in a subject related to information technology, although you may be able to enter this career if you have qualifications and experience in a business related area. Most training is on-the-job. However, some employers send their staff on external training courses such as those offered by the Institute for the Management of Information Systems (IMIS). Diploma and Higher Diploma courses are also available from the IMIS.

Qualifications: For entry to a degree course the minimum requirement is 3 Highers (A-C) plus Standard Grades (1-3) in 2 other subjects.

However, entry requirements vary between courses and alternative qualifications may be accepted—check prospectuses for details.

Database administrators are usually experienced systems designers or programmers. However, you may be able to enter this career if you have qualifications and experience in a business related area.

According to government statistics, employees in this type of job have the following qualifications. Higher Education: 5 out of 10 employees have their highest level of qualifications attained at degree level or equivalent or higher. Post-16 or Further Education: 2 out of 10 employees have their highest qualification at a level below a degree or higher degree or equivalent, but gained after the age of 16. School leaving age (16) qualifications or qualifications at SVQ3: 3 out of 10 employees gained their highest qualification at the age of 16 or have gained another qualification lower than a VQ level 3 since they were 16.

Computer Applications Programmer

Computer applications programmers write and test computer programmes. They deal with programmes that instruct computers to carry out specific tasks, *e.g.*, stock control. Many programmers spend time adapting existing programmes to suit clients.

Work Activities: Applications programmers write programmes that instruct a computer to perform tasks such as controlling company stock or updating staff records. They may write new programmes or, more commonly, adapt existing ones. For example, they may alter 'off-the-shelf' computer packages to meet the requirements of an individual firm. They may work on one programme or a number ('suite') of programmes.

Programmers who work for a large computer-using firm or organisation may be responsible for maintaining and updating one or more programmes. This requires them to solve any problems that individual users have and adapt the programme to fit in with any changes in the way they work.

When they write a new programme application, programmers follow a specification, or 'spec', provided by a systems analyst. The spec describes what the programme should do. It may be very precise, in which case the programmer has to follow it exactly, or it may be quite 'loose', which allows the programmer to be more creative. Each spec shows a series of steps, which the programmer translates into computer code. Once programmers have developed a new programme, they have to check it very carefully for faults ('bugs') and carefully test it using mock data before it is ready for the final user.

It is becoming more common for applications programmers to be responsible for duties that systems analysts have carried out in the past. Where this is the case, employers may use the title 'analyst programmer' for this career.

Applications programmers often work in teams, with each person contributing to the programme or suite of programmes.

Personal Qualities and Skills: You will need to be analytical and logical in your approach to problem solving. Attention to detail is essential. You will need to be patient because an important part of the work involves looking for faults in the programme.

Programmers must enjoy working on their own; you must be able to concentrate for long periods of time. You will also need good communication and teamwork skills because much of the work is project based. Good written communication skills are essential when compiling reports and writing user-friendly manuals.

Pay and Opportunities: Salaries for computer applications programmers vary depending on the range of their responsibilities and the size and type of company they work for. The pay rates given below are approximate. Salaries are in the range of £19,500—£25,500 a year, rising to £31,500—£38,000. Higher earners can make around £49,500 a year.

Salaries may include performance-related pay, profit sharing or company bonuses. Computer applications programmers usually work 35—37 hours Monday to Friday.

Applications programmers work for large computer-using organisations, software houses and computer manufacturers. Some experienced programmers work on a freelance basis—usually on short-term contracts. This work can be available through specialist IT recruitment agencies.

The following information is sourced from government statistics. The government's definition of types of job is slightly different to that used in this programme. For this type of job, the most relevant Government-defined occupation is 'Software professionals'.

In 2001 there were 17,200 people working as 'Software professionals' in Scotland. 80 in every 10,000 employees working in Scotland were employed as 'Software professionals'.

Estimates of projected future job openings requiring new entrants to the jobs market are available, but not at the level of detail of 'Software professionals'. It is estimated that over the five years between 2003 and 2008 there will be a need for 7,000 new employees to fill vacancies in the broader occupational type of 'Information & Communication Technology'. 1 out of every 20 employees works part time in this type of job.

Entry Routes and Training: Most entrants to this job have a degree or Higher National Diploma in a relevant subject. Information technology and computing courses are available at a large number of institutions.

It is becoming more common for employers to recruit graduates and people with HNDs in non-computing subjects who demonstrate relevant qualities, such as creativity and good communication skills. Relevant postgraduate courses are available.

In some cases, it may be possible to enter with Highers and train on the job, although this is becoming less common. Relevant SVQs are available up to level 4.

Qualifications: For entry to a degree course the minimum requirement is 3 Highers (A-C) plus Standard Grades (1-3) in 2 other subjects.

However, entry requirements vary between courses and alternative qualifications may be accepted—check prospectuses for details.

According to government statistics, employees in this type of job have the following qualifications. Higher Education: 7 out of 10 employees have their highest level of qualifications attained at degree level or equivalent or higher. Post-16 or Further Education: 2 out of 10 employees have their highest qualification at a level below a degree or higher degree or equivalent, but gained after the age of 16. School leaving age (16) qualifications or qualifications at SVQ3: 2 out of 10 employees gained their highest qualification at the age of 16 or have gained another qualification lower than a VQ level 3 since they were 16.

Adult Opportunities: There is no formal upper age limit for entry into this occupation.

Employers tend to look for experience in older applicants; therefore, new entrants are advised to gain experience in computer help desk or similar work before moving on to applications programmer posts.

If you are a graduate with a non-relevant degree, entry is still possible with some employers. However, taking a one-year information technology postgraduate conversion course will improve your chances.

Suitable applicants aged 21 or over may do a college or university Access course. No formal qualifications are required to enter an Access course, but you should check individual course details. They lead to relevant degree/HND courses.

Another option would be a Higher National Certificate in Computing on a part-time basis, either evening and/or daytime.

Alternatively, taking short intensive courses in specific computing languages, such as C, C++ and Java, with private accredited IT training providers can help you to develop the portfolio of technical skills needed by employers. Courses are available on a flexible, evening, weekend or day part-time basis.

Distance learning opportunities include the Open University, offering a degree in Computing and Mathematical Sciences and a diploma in Computing.

Many educational institutions offer specific qualifications on a distance/online learning basis.

Computeach offers courses in C++, Visual Basic and Java, plus a Sponsorship for degree level study of Computing can be available through some of the larger IT companies.

Computer Network Manager

Computer network managers support and maintain the computer networks used in many organisations. A network is a group of computers linked together, usually through a powerful central computer called a fileserver.

Work Activities: Computer network managers maintain and support the computer networks used in many large organisations. A network is a group of computers linked with one another, usually via a powerful central computer known as a fileserver. Networking offers a number of potential advantages for organisations, for example:

- The staff of the organisation can share information and resources.
- Staff teams can work collaboratively on a project or document, even if they are based in several different offices.
- Data (*e.g.* total number of sales/enquiries) can be collected and analysed centrally.
- Equipment such as printers and scanners can be shared among a number of users.

Network managers have overall responsibility for one or more computer networks. Organisations often have several networks: for example, a local area network (LAN) within an office or department and a wide area network (WAN) linking all the organisation's branches across the UK or worldwide. Network managers perform (or instruct their staff to perform) routine tasks such as connecting new users to the network, issuing passwords and removing log-ins for staff who have left. They make sure the network is secure and access can be obtained only by those with the appropriate authorisation.

An important responsibility is checking that regular backups are performed. At the end of the day (or overnight), all the current data on the network has to be saved on to a separate storage device such as a magnetic disk or tape. This is then kept in a secure place well away from the main fileserver. In the event of an accident or network failure the following day, all data up to the previous night can be restored from the backup.

When there are problems with the network, computer network managers investigate and try to resolve them as quickly as possible. To do this they may need to work with hardware and software suppliers and specialist agencies such as internet access providers. Computer network managers are also involved in resourcing and forward planning, including updating network hardware and software in accordance with the organisation's current and predicted needs.

Managers may also have to visit other offices and sites, *e.g.* when installing or updating network hardware and software.

Computer network managers typically supervise a small team of network administrators, technicians and support workers. They have an in-depth knowledge of computer systems, as well as business knowledge and some programming skills.

Personal Qualities and Skills: As a computer network manager, you should have an interest in computers and a detailed knowledge of network hardware and software.

You will need a patient, methodical approach, as identifying the cause of a problem sometimes requires a degree of detective work. For managing staff and liaising with users and suppliers, good written and spoken communication skills are important.

When problems arise, network managers may have to work outside normal office hours. They may also be 'on call' at other times in case there is an emergency such as a systems failure. Network managers need to be calm and conscientious. They must be able to cope with a degree of stress, especially when the network is not functioning correctly.

For some jobs, you may need a driving licence.

Pay and Opportunities: The pay rates given below are approximate. Salaries are in the range of £25,000—£32,000 a year, rising to £42,500—£57,000. Higher earners can make around £76,000 a year. Salaries may include performance-related pay, profit sharing or company bonuses.

Computer network managers work a basic 37-hour week, Monday to Friday. Late finishes and weekend work may be required and they may be called out to deal with emergencies.

Jobs exist throughout the UK with employers in industry and commerce, including banks, building societies and insurance companies and in the public sector with local and central government departments, the NHS and public utilities. Some experienced IT managers work on a freelance basis—usually on short term contracts.

The following information is sourced from government statistics. The government's definition of types of job is slightly different to that used in this programme. For this type of job, the most relevant Government-defined occupation is 'Information and communication technology managers'.

In 2001 there were 9,400 people working as 'Information and communication technology managers' in Scotland. 43 in every 10,000 employees working in Scotland were employed as 'Information and communication technology managers'.

Estimates of projected future job openings requiring new entrants to the jobs market are available, but not at the level of detail of 'Information and communication technology managers'. It is estimated that over the five years between 2003 and 2008 there will be a need for 21,000 new employees to fill vacancies in the broader occupational type of 'Functional Managers'.

1 out of every 20 employees works part time in this type of job.

Entry Routes and Training: Most computer network managers hold a relevant degree or Higher National Diploma qualification.

Different courses have different emphases and it is important to check the prospectuses of the institutions concerned to identify those courses most likely to meet your future career aspirations. For network management, relevant topics would include computer systems architecture, data communications/ networking and systems analysis and design. Network management is not normally an entry-level job, however and you would usually expect to gain experience in a role such as systems analyst or network administrator before obtaining a position as network manager.

Many network managers study part time for further qualifications, *e.g.* the professional qualifications of the British Computer Society (BCS) and the Institute for the Management of Information Systems (IMIS). These can be studied full time or part time, by distance learning or at a local college.

They may also study for qualifications relevant to the specific networks and systems used in their organisation, for example, Microsoft Certified Network Engineer (MCNE) or Certified Novell Engineer (CNE). Studying for these qualifications typically involves attending short, intensive courses at specially accredited training centres.

Qualifications: Most computer network managers are graduates. Employers are also likely to want you to have experience in a role such as systems analyst or network administrator.

For entry to a degree course the minimum requirement is 3 Highers (A-C) plus Standard Grades in 2 other subjects.

However, entry requirements vary between courses and alternative qualifications may be accepted—check prospectuses for details.

According to government statistics, people working in this type of job have the following qualifications. Higher Education: 6 out of 10 employees have their highest level of qualifications attained at degree level or equivalent or higher. Post-16 or

Further Education: 2 out of 10 employees have their highest qualification at a level below a degree or higher degree or equivalent, but gained after the age of 16. School leaving age (16) qualifications or qualifications at SVQ3: 3 out of 10 employees gained their highest qualification at the age of 16 or have gained another qualification lower than a VQ level 3 since they were 16.

Computer System Analyst

Systems analysts design computer systems to help organisations work more quickly and efficiently. They work closely with staff at all levels to find out what problems people have with the existing system and what they hope a new system will achieve. Analysts produce a specification for a system that will meet the organisation's needs.

Work Activities: Systems analysts use information technology (IT) to help organisations work more quickly and efficiently. They investigate a business problem and then design a suitable computer system to improve they way the business works.

In many ways, systems analysts work as closely with people as they do with computers. At the start of a project, they talk to computer users and managers to find out what problems there are and what the organisation wants to achieve by investing in a new or improved system. For example, a business may want to reduce costs or increase the speed or scale of production.

The analyst carries out a detailed study of the organisation, its procedures and the needs of the people who use its systems. To do this, they need business knowledge, together with an understanding of computing and programming techniques. Systems analysts gather information by interviewing staff at all levels within the organisation.

Next, they look at this information and design a computer system (or a number of systems) that meets the organisation's needs. Analysts then write a system specification, describing how the new system will work, the new equipment the organisation will need to buy and the level of training staff will need. Once an organisation's management has picked and approved the system it likes, the systems analyst starts to work closely with IT specialists, systems designers and programmers to create the system. Systems analysts are more likely to update or redesign an out-of-date system rather than introduce a totally new one.

Although systems analysts often have an office from which they work, they usually have to travel to visit organisations that need their skills. They may also travel to meet representatives from companies that supply IT equipment.

Personal Qualities and Skills: To be a systems analyst, you must enjoy solving problems and weighing up the pros and cons of different solutions. You will need a logical, analytical and investigative mind, together with creative abilities. You must have a good general awareness of business, as well as the ability and willingness to find out about the particular organisation that needs your help.

Strong communication skills are just as important as technical knowledge. You must be able to work closely with staff at all levels throughout an organisation, including managers and IT specialists but also the people who will use the system day-to-day. You will need good listening skills and the ability to ask the right questions, in order to find out what problems people have with the existing system and what their expectations are for the future.

You may need tact, diplomacy and good negotiating skills, perhaps to convince staff to allow computers to take over aspects of their job, or persuade a manager that the system you have suggested is the best available. You must be able to explain your ideas clearly and concisely. Good report writing skills are very important.

Pay and Opportunities: Salaries for computer systems analysts vary depending on the range of their responsibilities and the size and type of company they work for. The pay rates given below are approximate. Salaries are in the range of £19,500—£25,500 a year, rising to £31,500—£38,000. Higher earners can make around £49,500 a year. Salaries may include performance related pay, profit sharing or company bonuses.

Systems analysts usually work 35—37 hours, Monday to Friday.

Jobs exist throughout the UK with employers in industry and commerce, including banks, building societies and insurance companies and in the public sector with local and central government departments, the NHS and public utilities. Systems analysis is increasingly carried out on a short-term contract or consultancy basis. This can be undertaken through specialist IT recruitment agencies.

The following information is sourced from government statistics. The government's definition of types of job is slightly different to that used in this programme. For this type of job, the most relevant Government-defined occupation is 'Software professionals'.

In 2001 there were 17,200 people working as 'Software professionals' in Scotland. 80 in every 10,000 employees working in Scotland were employed as 'Software professionals'.

Estimates of projected future job openings requiring new entrants to the jobs market are available, but not at the level of detail of 'Software professionals'. It is estimated that over the five years between 2003 and 2008 there will be a need for 7000 new employees to fill vacancies in the broader occupational type of 'Information & Communication Technology'.

1 out of every 20 employees works part time in this type of job.

Entry Routes and Training: Most entrants are graduates. While a degree in an information technology related subject might be an advantage, some employers recruit graduates of any subject and provide all the necessary IT training.

It is common to enter this role after gaining a number of years' programming experience.

Qualifications: Most computer systems analysts are graduates. Employers are also likely to want you to have several years' experience of working in an IT department.

For entry to a degree course the minimum requirement is 3 Highers (A-C) plus Standard Grades (1-3) in 2 other subjects.

However, entry requirements vary between courses and alternative qualifications may be accepted—check prospectuses for details.

It may be possible to become a systems analyst if you have a degree in a non IT related subject, if you have experience of project management.

According to government statistics, employees in this type of job have the following qualifications. Higher Education: 7 out of 10 employees have their highest level of qualifications attained at degree level or equivalent or higher. Post-16 or Further Education: 2 out of 10 employees have their highest qualification at a level below a degree or higher degree or equivalent, but gained after the age of 16. School leaving age (16) qualifications or qualifications at SVQ3: 2 out of 10 employees gained their highest qualification at the age of 16 or have gained another qualification lower than a VQ level 3 since they were 16.

Computer System Programmer

Computer systems programmers write programmes to control the internal operations of computers. This involves designing programmes that are efficient, fast and versatile. They spend a lot of time testing their programmes.

Work Activities: Systems programmers research, design and develop programmes that control the internal operations of computers. Following specifications provided by the systems analyst, the programmer writes programmes that are fast, versatile and efficient. Their aim is to make computer systems (both hardware and software) work more efficiently. This includes looking at how computers handle data and text, send information to printers and link up to telecommunications systems.

Programmers may begin each project by producing a flow chart or diagram to break down the project into a series of steps, which the programmer then follows in a logical order. The programmer translates these steps into instructions written in computer language. This is a very technical job; systems programmers deal with complicated computer language.

Programmers spend a lot of time testing and improving the programme and removing faults ('debugging'). Systems programmers produce flow charts and programme notes to help technical writers, who are responsible for producing user manuals.

Apart from computers, all sorts of equipment have operating systems, including printers, electronic personal organisers and telecommunications equipment. Systems programmers may work for companies that produce these items; they write or adapt operating systems.

Personal Qualities and Skills: As a systems programmer, you will need strong technical knowledge of complex computer languages. You also need good written skills, to produce reports, diagrams and instructions for other members of the team. You must be a good problem solver with a logical and methodical approach to your work. Patience and attention to detail are vital qualities. The ability to cope well when things go wrong is very important.

Pay and Opportunities: The pay rates given below are approximate. Salaries for computer systems programmers are in the range of £19,500—£25,500 a year, rising to £31,500—£38,000. Higher earners can make around £49,500 a year. Salaries may include performance-related pay, profit sharing or company bonuses.

Systems programmers usually work 35—37 hours Monday to Friday.

Jobs exist throughout the UK with software houses, consultancies, computer manufacturers and large-scale computer users. Some fixed-term contract work is available for those with substantial experience. This can be undertaken through specialist IT recruitment agencies.

The following information is sourced from government statistics. The government's definition of types of job is slightly different to that used in this programme. For this type of job, the most relevant Government-defined occupation is 'Software professionals'.

In 2001 there were 17,200 people working as 'Software professionals' in Scotland. 80 in every 10,000 employees working in Scotland were employed as 'Software professionals'. Estimates of projected future job openings requiring new entrants to the jobs market are available, but not at the level of detail of 'Software professionals'. It is estimated that over the five years between 2003 and 2008 there will be a need for 7000 new employees to fill vacancies in the broader occupational type of 'Information & Communication Technology'.

1 out of every 20 employees works part time in this type of job.

Entry Routes and Training: Almost all entrants to this work have a degree in a relevant subject, although you may be able to enter with an Higher National Diploma. Information technology and computing courses are available at a large number of institutions.

Qualifications: For entry to a degree course the minimum requirement is 3 Highers (A-C) plus Standard Grades (1-3) in 2 other subjects.

However, entry requirements vary between course and alternative qualifications may be accepted—check prospectuses for details.

You may also be able to enter this career with a Higher National Diploma.

According to government statistics, employees in this type of job have the following qualifications. Higher Education: 7 out of 10 employees have their highest level of qualifications attained at degree level or equivalent or higher. Post-16 or Further Education: 2 out of 10 employees have their highest qualification at a level below a degree or higher degree or equivalent, but gained after the age of 16. School leaving age (16) qualifications or qualifications at SVQ3: 2 out of 10 employees gained their highest qualification at the age of 16 or have gained another qualification lower than a VQ level 3 since they were 16.

Computer Software Engineer

Computer software engineers analyse, design and create computer systems and software (the programmes used by a computer). Software engineers work on complex software, such as operating systems and the software used to control automated equipment used, for example, in production and manufacturing industries.

Work Activities: Computer software engineers traditionally work on the most complex types of software, including operating systems, while analyst/applications programmers work on software used to carry out business activities, such as managing a payroll. However, these career titles are becoming increasingly used to describe both types of work.

Software engineers are involved in all stages in the development of a software product. They apply software technology to meet a defined need or solve a particular problem. This could involve analysing an existing system, setting out how the new system will work and what features it will have (its specification), designing the system and then giving it a code that the computer can understand. Software engineers must test this code to make sure the computer can run it smoothly.

At the start of a project, software engineers have to develop their knowledge of the client's business and their particular needs and problems. Next, they work with their clients to agree on important issues such as the hardware and software they need, costs and deadlines, as well as setting out a proposal for what the finished software product should be. Software engineers (usually working in a team on larger programmes) will then begin to write the programme or programmes. They will then test the programme for bugs (faults), correcting any problems that they find.

Software engineers may train their clients to use the new programme or system. They are also likely to train any people who need to know how to support and maintain the system, for example, computer service technicians and support services engineers.

Computer software engineers may write instructions or manuals to go with the software they have developed.

Personal Qualities and Skills: Attention to detail and commitment to seeing projects through from start to finish are vital qualities. You must enjoy solving problems and have a logical, methodical approach to your work.

Computer software engineers need a high level of technical expertise. You must be willing to keep up-to-date with advances in technology, both in hardware and software.

Computer software engineers also need excellent interpersonal skills to work in teams and to communicate well with clients. You will usually need good written skills to present proposals and reports to clients and to write instructions and manuals for the programmes. Strong communication skills are also needed to train clients in how to use new programmes.

You must have a good understanding of the nature of your client's business activities and their information technology needs. As well as working in teams, software engineers must be able to work independently.

Software engineers often work to deadlines, so you must be well organised and able to work well under pressure.

Pay and Opportunities: Salaries for engineers vary. The pay rates given below are approximate. Software engineers earn £20,000—£25,500 a year, rising to £31,500—£38,000 . Higher earners can make around £49,500 a year.

Software engineers usually work 35 hours, Monday to Friday, with occasional late evenings when required to meet deadlines.

Most employment opportunities are in the aerospace, computing, instrumentation or telecommunications industries. Other employers are information technology consultants and software or systems houses.

The following information is sourced from government statistics. The government's definition of types of job is slightly different to that used in this programme. For this type of job, the most relevant government-defined occupation is 'Software professionals'.

In 2001 there were 17,200 people working as 'Software professionals' in Scotland. 80 in every 10,000 employees working in Scotland were employed as 'Software professionals'.

Estimates of projected future job openings requiring new entrants to the jobs market are available, but not at the level of detail of 'Software professionals'. It is estimated that over the five years between 2003 and 2008 there will be a need for 7,000 new employees to fill vacancies in the broader occupational type of 'Information & Communication Technology'. 1 out of every 20 employees works part time in this type of job.

Entry Routes and Training: Most software engineers have a degree or Higher National Diploma, although this does not always have to be in a computing subject. Many entrants have degrees in Software Engineering, Electronics or Computer Science. Some people have postgraduate qualifications in computing, in which case their first degrees need not be in computing subjects.

Degree courses may last three, four or five years full time or can be studied on a sandwich basis. Employers are increasingly interested in well-rounded graduates and it is possible to combine computing subjects with other subjects such as modern languages, business studies and electronics.

Computer software engineers can gain Chartered Engineer or Incorporated Engineer status, which is highly regarded by employers throughout industry.

To register with the Engineering Council as a Chartered or Incorporated Engineer, you must apply through an appropriate engineering professional institution.

To register as a Chartered Engineer, the usual route is to complete an accredited degree, as listed on the Engineering Council (UK) website, *e.g.* an MEng.

To register as an Incorporated Engineer (IEng), the usual route is to complete an accredited degree, as listed on the Engineering Council (UK) website, *e.g.* a B.Eng.

After gaining your degree, you will undergo Initial Professional Development (IPD). This involves accredited training and responsible experience in the workplace. This is followed by a Professional Review with interview to assess your competence and commitment to Continued Professional Development (CPD).

Qualifications: The usual entry requirement is a degree. It is also possible, however, to enter after completion of a Higher National Diploma or Higher National Certificate. The usual entry requirements for a degree in Software Engineering are 3/4 Highers (A-C) plus Standard Grades in 1/2 other subjects. At Higher, Maths and a science subject are often preferred and may be essential. At Standard Grade, English may be essential. Maths at Standard Grade is often required if not offered at Higher.

The usual entry requirements for an HNC/HND are 1/3 Highers and Standard Grades.

However, entry requirements vary between courses and alternative qualifications may be accepted—check prospectuses for details.

According to government statistics, employees in this type of job have the following qualifications. Higher Education: 7 out of 10 employees have their highest level of qualifications attained at degree level or equivalent or higher. Post-16 or Further Education: 2 out of 10 employees have their highest qualification at a level below a degree or higher degree or equivalent, but gained after the age of 16. School leaving age (16) qualifications or qualifications at SVQ3: 2 out of 10 employees gained their highest qualification at the age of 16 or have gained another qualification lower than a VQ level 3 since they were 16.

Information Scientist

Information scientists deal with information storage and retrieval. They may also produce information systems and conduct research work into areas such as how information is generated, stored and used. The work is often computer based.

Work Activities: Information scientists deal with information storage and retrieval. They need to store information, find particular information requested by their employer or a client and distribute the information to the employer or client in a way that is easy to understand. Sources of information include audiovisual materials, books, CD-ROMs, databases and reports. They may produce information systems, or carry out research work. They may research how information is generated, stored and used. A lot of research is computer based and deals with specialist areas such as computer-indexing or storing chemical formulae.

The work of an information scientist shares features with that of a librarian. Graduates from both information science and librarianship fill information posts. However, information scientists tend to work in smaller units handling specialist information. Also, they usually deal more with the dissemination than the storage of information.

Personal Qualities and Skills: You may need to be familiar with a scientific, technical, legal, commercial or other specialist field, so you need to keep up to date with research in that field as well as in information science. You also need to be aware of the information needs of your client(s) to develop suitable information systems. It is also important to be able to analyse and present complex information. Information scientists have to be competent computer users.

Pay and Opportunities: Salaries for information scientists vary depending on the sector they work in, the employer and the level of responsibility. Salaries are similar to those of librarians. The pay rates given below are approximate. Information scientists earn in the range of £18,000—£25,000 a year, rising to £30,000—£45,000. Higher rates are possible for some senior grades in government departments.

Information scientists usually work 35 hours Monday to Friday. However, where offices are open longer, you may need to work evenings and weekends. Some part-time opportunities are available.

Information scientists work for a wide range of employers throughout the UK and abroad, in commerce, industry, science and technology, electronic publishing, finance, law and education.

Several recruitment agencies offer short-term contracts working in this field. Freelance and consulting work is normally possible only after substantial work experience.

The following information is sourced from government statistics. The government's definition of types of job is slightly different to that used in this programme. For this type of job, the most relevant Government-defined occupation is 'Librarians'.

In 2001 there were 2,000 people working as 'Librarians' in Scotland. 9 in every 10,000 employees working in Scotland were employed as 'Librarians'.

Entry Routes and Training: You need a degree to enter information science. Several degrees in Information Science and Information and Library Studies are available.

A number of postgraduate courses are also available. Entry requirements for postgraduate courses vary. Some courses will accept you with a degree in any subject while others are more specific. Graduates with first degrees in science, technology, economics or other relevant subjects may be preferred. You will usually need pre-course work experience.

A limited number of financial awards are available for some postgraduate courses. The Institute of Information Scientists produces a list of such courses.

Once employed, you can take an SVQ level 4 in Information and Library Service.

Qualifications: For entry to a degree course in Information and Library Studies, the minimum requirement is 3 Highers plus 2 Standard Grades in other subjects. A Higher in English is usually required.

However, entry requirements vary between courses and alternative qualifications may be accepted—check prospectuses for details.

Bachelor of Science in Computer Science

The online Bachelor of Science in Computer Science degree will prepare you for a career in systems analysis and design, computer programming, project management, or management information systems. As a student, you will develop skills and knowledge in the areas of computer architecture, object-oriented analysis and design, software engineering, work-flow analysis and business processes. A total of 128 credit hours are required to earn a Bachelor of Science Degree in Computer Science. ($340 per credit hour)

A Career in Information Technology

Information technologies, including Internet technologies, have changed out lives significantly and will continue to have a huge impact on all kinds of careers, occupations and professions. So it follows that careers in Information Technology (IT) have enormous scope and variety.

A lot of jobs that are advertised today hadn't been thought of ten years ago, when Java was just an island and chat was something you did on the phone. The advent of broadband, the growth in home networking, 3G mobiles, digital downloads and the perennial quest for ever more advanced computer systems, means the variety of and scope of IT careers continues to grow.

IT Jobs—Technology Jobs—IT Career

As complex as information technology has become, however, figuring out how to best position yourself in the IT jobs lucrative capital stream that accompanies it may be even more difficult. Technology jobs are abundant in a growing economy so keep your resources close at hand.

Here is where Surrex comes in. While you focus on building your craft, we focus on the market trends you need to succeed in this highly competitive industry. We can tap you into an extensive, continuously updated database of current Information Technology jobs. Whether you wish to join our team of Information Technology consultants, or are looking for a Direct Hire position, we can assist you in finding exactly the right fit for you. We take into account your experience, skills and preferences in matching you with precisely the Information Technology jobs that will be of maximum, mutual benefit to you and your employer alike.

The most successful IT candidates visit our site on a regular basis to access the most up-to-date information about IT jobs and the developing trends of the Information Technology industry.

The following are just a few of the valuable, regularly updated resources Surrex offers the Information Technology job searcher:

The Changing IT Landscape: This is a short column written by Surrex staff members about the latest trends of the IT technology industry. Check back often to gain valuable tips, statistics and analysis about lucrative directions certain fields in IT are heading.

Company Resources: Surrex helps you stay up-to-date about the major players in the Information Technology industry by providing the latest news, white papers, relevant links, forums, as well as information about IT job openings.

Information Technology Consulting Events: We are constantly receiving updates about special IT events, conferences and exposition that are invaluable to IT job searchers. Allow Surrex to keep you informed about important Information Technology gatherings that can help you boost your IT career.

The energetic and self-motivated IT professionals who tap into the vast network of Information Technology resources, information and tools through Surrex find themselves at a significant competitive advantage over the thousands of other IT job searchers in the market today.

Surrex has assisted countless individuals who have bookmarked our site and check back with us on a regular basis. They become more adept at conducting themselves with confidence in Information Technology job interviews. They compose resumes with a keen understanding of precisely what IT employers are looking for in a candidate today. In short, they learn to think of technology in terms of where the money is—as well as where their IT career is going.

IT career researching, whether by gaining access to an exclusive network of *IT job seekers* and employers, or just staying up-to-date on latest technologies and trends, the most savvy IT professionals rely upon Surrex to consistently lead them to the right place, at precisely the right time!

Process and Technology Group (PTG)

The PTG works with each business unit to identify its IT and process needs and to ensure that appropriate solutions are developed and implemented. More than just an internal consulting organization, the PTG is responsible for knowing the business and the technology and identifying opportunities to improve both. Our departments are Manufacturing & Supply Chain Systems, Product Development Systems, Global Consumer Systems and Management Systems.

Our Role:

- Deliver IT value
- Provide strategic consulting through expertise in Ford information systems
- Manage customer relationships and co-locate with business partners
- Direct IT's strategy, cycle plan, portfolio management and business processes
- Manage prioritization and funding, solution research and benchmarking and performance objectives and metrics

Application Development Services (ADS)

ADS is the engine behind our support of Ford Motor Company. We are responsible for software architecture, delivery, maintenance and support across the life cycle. From certification of delivery-related competencies to resource management, we are a hands-on part of the excitement at Ford.

ADS is made up of four areas:

- *Practice:* Practice groups are comprised of IT professionals with deep personal application knowledge who deliver IT solutions supporting a specific business function. Most of the Practice groups are cross-functional teams assigned to a business process such as Product Development, Ford Customer Service Division, or Purchasing. They are responsible for software optimization, project and software change management, maintenance of systems integration and production management and support.
- *Competency Centres:* The Competency Centres are places of learning, career guidance and resource management organized around specific job families. For instance, there are competency centres for developers, project managers

and business analysts. They may be assigned as needed to a Practice team or to Architecture Management, or may work as part of a resource pool between projects. There is also a core staff to perform the management and operations of the Competency Center. The Competency Center allows flexible staffing, effective resource management and the development of core IT professional competencies.

- *Enterprise Architecture Management:* This is an execution-focused group of IT professionals who introduce cutting-edge technologies into IT and manage business processes. This group is both cross-functional and cross-competency in nature. They are responsible for forward-looking research and development, solution architecture and competitive intelligence. They are valuable consulting resources for Practice teams in all areas of the company, for example.
- *Technical Programme Management:* This cross-functional group is process-metrics focused. Some of their areas of expertise and responsibility include system development methodologies, process quality assurance and support for Six Sigma projects. Programme management disciplines, programme health assessment and manager certification are also handled by this group.

Student Programmes—Summer Intern Programme

This programme introduces you to Ford Motor Company's top-rated computer systems and how they are used throughout the company. You see first-hand how systems are developed and strategically implemented at Ford Motor Company. Challenging assignments not only broaden your work experience, but also help you understand the issues facing a global corporation. The programme also gives you the opportunity to:

- apply academic knowledge to real-world business situations
- learn more about information technology and process re-engineering

- make an informed decision on whether Ford Motor Company is the right place for you to start your career

Preferred Background: The programme is designed for students who have completed their sophomore year and are majoring in computer science, management information systems or other technical areas. We look for strong academic credentials and a keen interest in applying information technology and process re-engineering in the automotive products and services industry. Strong communications skills and the ability to work on a team in a fast-past, ever-changing environment are a plus.

Intern Assignments: As a summer intern, you'll take on assignments that build your skills in areas such as process re-engineering, systems design and development, Web development, systems maintenance and support and hardware and infrastructure support. In addition, you will gain experience working in a dynamic team environment with deliverables and deadlines. You will be given the opportunity to demonstrate innovation and creativity, oral and written communication skills and negotiation skills.

Your work will be measurable, so that you can track your progress and see if you have accomplished your objectives. You will have the opportunity to learn and contribute to the organization and you will feel a real sense of ownership in your project. You will improve your understanding of Ford Motor Company, its products, people and vision. The knowledge you take with you will help you in whatever career path you choose.

Members of our Ford College Graduate programme will be available to help you during your three-month assignment, to familiarize you with the company, our culture and life in Southeast Michigan.

If you are graduating in the 12 months after your internship, you will be considered for full-time employment as a Ford College Graduates (FCG).

Full Time Employment—Ford College Graduate Programme

This two-year developmental programme gives you a solid foundation for your career with experience in different areas.

You plan your programme with your advisor and executive sponsor. You can expect three to five assignments in information technology either at Ford Motor Company or Ford Financial. You'll also plan one or two cross-functional assignments in a business operation such as Product Development, Manufacturing, Marketing or Purchasing. As you gain experience, your primary responsibilities are to contribute to the company and learn as much as possible about our business, leadership behaviours and technology.

Preferred Background: To qualify, you should be in the top 25 percent of your class and have an interest in applying information technology and process reengineering techniques in the automotive industry. We prefer a degree in Computer Science, Information Systems or other technical area, or an M.B.A. with a technical undergraduate degree.

Your Advisor: During your programme, your advisor will coach and counsel you and help to plan your career development to satisfy your interests and the business needs of the company. As your mentor, the advisor not only enhances your learning and broadens your professional and leadership experiences but also has a unique opportunity to secure our future success by developing our new employees.

Your Executive Sponsor: Your executive sponsor is a member of the Information Technology operating committee who helps you with overall career planning and identifying areas for development. With a focus on long-term career planning, your sponsor counsels you for the first seven years of your career. Together, you and your sponsor develop a five-year development plan, identifying career opportunities and technologies that interest you.

Your Rotations: Together with your advisor, you will develop a preliminary rotation plan. Rotational assignments provide an understanding of how Information Technology supports Ford Motor Company's business processes, a greater understanding of Ford Motor Company, enhancement of your business and technical skills and a basis for future career choices.

Assignment Supervisors: For each rotation, a supervisor will be responsible for establishing your work objectives, developing training plans, conducting performance reviews and providing ongoing coaching and counselling. Your supervisor clarifies your responsibilities and provides day-to-day guidance to help you learn from and contribute to your department.

Training: Ford College Graduates participate in a seven-week hands-on New Hire Orientation programme designed to give you a proper introduction to Information Technology and Ford Motor Company. You are also eligible to take certain courses designed as recommended core training, regardless of your primary area of specialty.

FCG Council: Our Information Technology FCG Council organizes forums that meet on a regular basis to promote networking and communication among FCGs in the various IT components. The group also assists with such activities as recruiting, new hire orientation and ongoing support of the FCG Programme.

Full Time Employment—Experienced Hire Programme

Need a new challenge? Consider Ford Motor Company. If you think of Ford as part of the old economy, a Rust Belt behemoth drowning in its own bureaucracy, it's time to think again! We are evolving into one of the world's leading consumer companies for automotive products and services and advanced technology is vital to our success.

Do you think you can master Ford Motor Company's top-rated information systems? We have overwhelming computing power, with one of the world's largest numerically intensive computing centres. Do you think you can understand how it is used throughout the company? We need you to define and implement strategic solutions that leverage technology and deliver significant business value. Challenging assignments are the norm and you gain an understanding of the issues facing one of the largest global corporations. A position with Ford will require you to deliver information technology solutions that transform the business.

Preferred Background: We are looking for people experienced in computer science, management information systems and other technical areas. You need to have a keen interest in applying information technology and process re-engineering to transform the company into the premier consumer company for automotive products and services. In addition to applying your technical and process skills, you will work in a dynamic team environment. Strong communication skills and the ability to work on a global team in a fast-paced, ever-changing environment are also part of Information Technology jobs.

We need you to use your skills in areas such as consulting, process re-engineering, systems design and development, web development, systems maintenance and support and hardware and infrastructure support. You will be expected to demonstrate innovation and creativity, superior oral and written communication skills and negotiation skills.

Manager Careers and Jobs

Employment Information: Career and Job Highlights for Computer and Information Systems Managers:

- Occupation growth is expected to increase as resulting from wider computer jobs
- The most qualified individuals for management positions will have formal previous education and work training
- Highly qualified individuals will also have a Master's degree in information systems management or business related field.

Computer Programming

Careers, Jobs and Training: Computer Programming Career and Job Highlights:

- In 2002, the majority of employed computer programmers had received a bachelor's degree. About 20 % had received a master's degree or doctorate degree.
- Compared to other fields, computer-programming jobs are anticipated to grow at a slower rate in the future.

- The most competitive candidates for employment will have many necessary and related programming skills.

Computer Programming Career

Computer programmers develop the instructions and languages computers use to operate. They also resolve computer problems and logical tests within the system. The roles of programmers and programmes have evolved with technical advancements in language and computing. The responsibilities and backgrounds of engineers vary depending on the company or agency.

Essentially, computer programmes instruct the computer on how to function. These functions differ according to the information required. The time it takes to write a programme ranges between a few hours for simple programmes to years for more complex programmes. Many programmers collaborate in a team in this process.

Programmers take the designs of software engineers and turn them into functional computer instructions that make up a programme. This process includes using technical language codes that vary according to the program's use. Many different languages are used, including those that are platform-specific for databases, Many programmers know more than a single language and they are identified according to they type of function or language they do know.

Often, programmers will change existing codes and programmes. When they do this they place comments into the instructions to make other users aware of the changes. Computer-assisted software engineering (CASE) assist engineers in this process by automatically creating large coded sections. Preexisting code is also stored in libraries to allow more convenient and productive customizing.

Programmers run programmes to test and re-test them for errors. They then correct and "debug" the problems, a process that may span the program's entire life. Programmers that work within a mainframe system write instructions for a central operator or write manuals for programme users.

Programmers are categorized as either applications programmers or systems programmers. Applications programmers develop or modify programmes for a specific purpose, such as recording a companies' inventory. Systems programmers work in a much broader field, developing computer, networking and operating systems.

These types of programmers alter the instructions given to networks and other systems units to enable them to effectively communicate with other hard equipment, including disk drives and terminals. Systems programmers have a fundamental knowledge of whole systems, enabling them to resolve programming problems that applications programmer often face. Presently, the most common form of programming in the computer services industry occurs for the rising popularity of software packages.

Software development programmers often work with other specialists in creating either customized or packaged general-use software. This includes games, financial management and other programmes used for educational purposes.

Some smaller organizations employ programmer-analysts who do both programming and analysis on systems. Both users and programmers alike are finding that new languages and programming resources are becoming much more efficient. Many home PC users are assuming the responsibilities once commonly held by programmers. One example is spreadsheet and packaged financial software that allows personal users to operate programmes and complex calculations with relative ease.

In 2002, computer programmes accounted for about one-half million jobs. Most industries employ programmers, but the greater number are found in software publishing and systems design service industries. Many telecommunications, manufacturing, management, educational, governmental and financial firms employ a large amount of programmers as well.

Many computer programmers work independently as contractors or consultants for companies needing specialized knowledge in areas of computer languages and application. An organization, such as a marketing firm, may contract with an independent programmer or an agency to provide debugging services in order to begin running any kind of management software application. Hiring programmers through contractual agreements rather than as permanent employees is an efficient way of harnessing people with the specific skills needed without having to train or retrain newcomers. Contractual agreements range from a few weeks to more than a year.

Computer Programming Training and Job Qualifications: Educational experience is becoming a more common need among employees with the rise in skilled and specialized job candidates. The most qualified applicants will have a bachelor's degree or, at the minimum, a certificate of a two-year computer programming degree. Many new computer programmers entering the field hold associate degrees and many colleges and institutes offer this kind of degree in related computer information and science-related fields.

Employers typically seek computer programmers with specialized experience in a particular area. Graduatescan enrol in courses at a technical or college institution to gain specialized training in a certain area. Although having a college degree is very helpful, more employers are preferring candidates with practical working experience or possessing a vocational computer programming degree.

Many programmers have a degree in a computer science field, while some have simply enrolled in courses as educational supplements. As employers require more training and education, there should be a substantially higher number of programmers with college educations and degrees.

The need for a particular set of skills varies according to the different fields, whether it is in engineering, mathematics, scientific, or business applications. Emerging programming languages are creating a competitive field of applicants with the relevant knowledge. Candidates with skills in special languages that involve such technical features as graphic user interface (GUI) are highly demanded. Also, highly qualified job applicants will have business and management skills. These and other skills can be acquired through internships or on-campus work programmes.

Systems programmers typically have a bachelor's degree to complement an expansive knowledge of computer science. These programmers should be able to configure database (including Oracle, Sybase and DB2) and operating systems within different organizations.

The most qualified applicants for programming jobs will have analytical and logical thinking skills along with patience and creativity in designing better programmes. Software programmes are often very sophisticated and abstract and thus systems programmers should also be able to exercise strong problem-solving and technical skill. The ability to effectively communicate within a team is also preferable among employers.

Amateur programmers just beginning their career may work alone or within a team, depending on the difficulty of the project. Some kind of supervision is always required at first and programmers should constantly modernize their knowledge of new technology through offered courses.

Advancements opportunities for programmers include becoming a chief manager or supervisor. This depends on the respective programmer's current skills and knowledge level. Programmers with the acquired skills and education may also move between specialized fields, such as systems, management, or research or media technology. These and opportunities, including consulting opportunities, should grow as employers continue to hire programmers in specialized areas.

Job applicants can enhance their qualifications by becoming certified in programming. In addition to gaining certification through voluntary means, different programmes exist including those offered by software and product companies.

Computer Programming Job and Employment Opportunities: Programming job increase is projected to grow at an equal rate with other jobs over the next decade. Experts predict that computer sectors in which design and software services are related will be among the most rapid growing sectors during this time period. Programmers will grow in demand, as evolving technologies require companies to adapt to new language and computer systems. Moreover, job turnover will create more openings for programming applicants.

Programming growth rates, however, are expected to not exceed the growth rate of specialists in other computer-related fields. Changing technology is changing the scope of programmers' responsibilities, as code writing can be accomplished through automated computer programmes without the need of manual work. This change in scope is also due to the growing use of software packages and the ability of users to write their own programmes. Technological advancement also means that firms will seek lower costs through out-sourcing jobs to foreign countries.

Despite these changes, businesses will remain to seek programmers for management and programming needs. Programmers will thus need to maintain their skills, especially as they relate to networks, wireless hardware and Internet and Intranet communications. The growth of these online communications should necessitate larger numbers of programmers to develop client/server, media, graphic user interface (GUI) and wireless operations. Also, programmers will continually be needed to implement technological security system with its growing use.

As programming becomes more complex, four-year college graduates will become more highly competitive. Those with skills in language programming—including languages for network, database and Internet management—will become highly favourable. Programmers seeking jobs should stay abreast of the current technologies that employer's need. They will also benefit in gaining practical experience to supplement that knowledge.

3

Other Related Jobs

Computer Science

Computer science programmes prepare people to work with computing problems and solutions. Students learn computer systems design. They study software and hardware design. They also learn to profile the needs of specific end-user situations.

It's become a cliche, that once you buy a computer, it's already outdated within about two weeks. Technology keeps advancing faster and faster. Computers that used to take up a whole room now fit into the palm of your hand! We now think of typewriters as artifacts from the dark ages! Today we live in the Information Age. Computer scientists take technology and bits of plastic to give us more ways to digitize our world.

With a degree in computer science, you can work as entry-level programmers and network administrators. You can work for all kinds of organizations, from small businesses to software start-ups to government agencies. After all, nearly every professional organization uses computers to keep things running. That means people are needed to keep the computers running themselves.

In computer science programmes, you might be surprised to learn that you take several math courses, including advanced algebra, statistics and calculus. This is because math is the basis for most computing languages. Of course, you take several computer science courses. This includes learning different programming languages, such as Java and C++. You take courses about computer networks, database management and operating systems (think Mac OS X or Windows 2000). You also learn how computers are built and how to develop new computer technology.

In addition, many programmes allow you to specialize in a specific area of computer science. These can include artificial intelligence, computer graphics and numerical analysis, to name a few.

Most four-year colleges and universities offer bachelor's degrees in computer science. Most community colleges offer two-year programmes that can be transferred to a four-year school.

Many schools offer graduate degree programmes in computer science. These programmes take from two to five years after you finish your bachelorÆs degree. Most people who get graduate degrees in computer science become high-level computer scientists or professors."

College Preparation: For this programme, schools recommend that you know how to use a computer and the Internet.

You can prepare for this programme by taking courses in high school that prepare you for college. This typically includes four years of English, three years of math, three years of social studies and two years of science. Some colleges also require two years of a second language.

- Network Technology
- Computer Science and Programming
- Advanced Algebra courses
- Calculus
- Probability and Statistics

Undergraduate Special

Many programmes require you to apply for admission even after you've been admitted to the school. Typically you must complete introductory computer science courses. You may also have to take courses in logic, calculus and physics.

Graduate Admissions

Admission to graduate programmes is competitive. You need a bachelor's degree in computer science or a similar field, good grades and good test scores

Additional requirements at some schools include:

- Graduate Record Exam (GRE) General
- Graduate Record Exam (GRE) Computer Science
- Letters of recommendation
- Personal statement

Typical Course Work

This undergraduate programme typically includes courses in the following subjects:

- Analysis of Algorithms
- Calculus
- Computer Architecture
- Computer Graphics
- Computer Networks
- Computer Organization
- Database Systems
- Introduction to Computer Science
- Operating Systems
- Programming Languages
- Software Engineering
- Statistics

Graduate programmes that lead to a master's or doctoral degree typically include:

- Required courses
- Thesis (master's degree)
- Preliminary exams (doctoral degree only)
- Dissertation and dissertation defense (doctoral degree)

Things to Know

Computer science programmes are often called "Computer Information and Science" or "Computer Science and

Engineering. Although it's true that a bachelor's degree in computer science will teach you a variety of skills that many employers value, it is becoming more common for employers to require a master's degree for many jobs. One reason might be that technology is becoming more complex. Therefore, you need more time to focus on a particular area.

Computational Mathematics

Computational mathematics programmes teach people to use math to design and build computers. Students also learn how to use computer technology to create models and simulated experiments. They also learn how to use algorithms and binary code.

If you're interested in several different scientific disciplines, computational mathematics might be a good choice of study for you. Computational mathematics is related to several other disciplines, including mathematics, computer science, physics, astronomy, astrophysics and geoscience. Computational mathematics teaches you to study and attempt to solve problems in science and engineering. For example, you can study turbulence in order to make air travel safer. You also learn computer-aided graphic design.

You can use your math, computing and engineering skills to work in a variety of fields. You can work for a computer hardware company, developing high-performance computer chips. Or, you can work for a genetic engineering lab, studying how DNA functions and develops.

In computational mathematics programmes, you take courses in several areas of math. This usually includes statistics, several kinds of mathematical analysis and computer modelling and simulation. Nearly all of your courses will include heavy use of computers, since many programmes use sophisticated software to teach mathematical concepts. In turn, students become skilled in using computers.

Several schools offer bachelor's degrees in computational mathematics. In some cases, you can minor in computational mathematics while getting your undergraduate degree in math or a related field. However, usually you get a bachelor's degree in math and then decide to specialize in computational mathematics during your master's studies. About 30 schools offer master's and doctoral degrees in computational mathematics. These programmes take from two to five years after you finish your bachelorÆs degree. Most people with graduate degrees in computational mathematics become professors and researchers."

College Preparation: For this programme, schools recommend that you know how to use a computer and the Internet.

You can prepare for this programme by taking courses in high school that prepare you for college. This typically includes four years of English, three years of math, three years of social studies and two years of science. Some colleges also require two years of a second language.

- Computer Science and Programming
- Physics
- Pre-Calculus
- Calculus
- Probability and Statistics

Graduate Admissions

Admission to graduate programmes is competitive. You need a bachelor's degree, good grades and good test scores

Additional requirements at some schools include:

- Graduate Record Exam (GRE) General
- Letters of recommendation
- Personal statement
- Undergraduate major or significant course work in math, including calculus, linear algebra and statistics

Typical Course Work

This undergraduate programme typically includes courses in the following subjects:

- Applied Analysis
- Complex Analysis

- Computational Linear Algebra
- Computer Programming
- Differential Equations
- Modelling
- Nonlinear Equations
- Numerical Analysis
- Optimization
- Probability and Statistics
- Real Analysis
- Wavelet and Multi-Resolution Analysis

Graduate programmes that lead to a master's or doctoral degree typically include:

- Required courses
- Thesis (master's degree)
- Preliminary exams (doctoral degree only)
- Dissertation and dissertation defense (doctoral degree)

Things to Know

Computational mathematics is often considered a subset of applied mathematics. Often, they are combined into a single degree programme.

Computer Engineering Technology

Computer engineering technology programmes prepare people to help engineers design and build computer systems. Students learn to install and maintain equipment. They also learn to write and test software programmes.

What does it mean to engineer a computer? You may imagine somebody tinkering with the chips and the connections inside a computer system to get it to run with maximum efficiency. And that's partly right.

But in many computer engineering technology programmes you spend much more time on software. That's because engineering is about applying the scientific method to solve practical problems, so it can be done to software as well as to hardware.

In this programme, you start by studying math and physics. Physics helps you understand the workings of electronic circuits. Just as important, it teaches you how to solve problems by experimenting, gathering data and testing theories. You take more specialized courses that teach you how circuits can represent logical operations. You learn what actually goes on inside those amazing chips. And you study how data is communicated over networks. You learn a few programming languages. You also study how popular kinds of software store and process data.

If your programme focuses on engineering technology, you study the logical processes that go on before any code is written; that is, you study how to solve a problem by creating an algorithm. You learn skills you will use in research and development. With two or three years of full-time study beyond high school, you can earn an associate degree in a programme of this kind. This will qualify you to work as a technician within an engineering team. A four-year programme will earn you a bachelor's degree and you can work as an engineering technologist. In some states, you may be able to work as an engineer. This programme is available at about 80 colleges.

Much more common are programmes that prepare you to work as a computer technician. You install and repair computer systems, networks and peripherals. You troubleshoot, consult manuals and online help, run tests and load software. You show workers how to use the computer equipment and software. About 300 colleges offer a two-year programme of this kind, leading to an associate degree."

College Preparation: You can prepare for this programme by taking courses in high school that prepare you for college. This typically includes four years of English, three years of math, three years of social studies and two years of science. Some colleges also require two years of a second language.

- Computer Science and Programming
- English Composition
- Biology
- Chemistry

- Physics
- Trigonometry

Typical Course Work

An associate degree programme in this field typically includes courses in the following subjects:

- College Algebra
- College Trigonometry
- English Composition
- Engineering Physics
- Electronic Circuits
- Digital Logic
- Introduction to Computer Science
- Programming in C++ and/or Visual Basic

A programme that emphasizes software also includes courses such as the following:

- Algorithm Design and Analysis
- Data Communications
- Machine and Assembly Language
- Networking and Internet Technologies

A programme that emphasizes hardware also includes courses such as the following:

- Computer-Assisted Circuit Design
- Microprocessor Technology
- Solid State Devices

A bachelor's degree programme in this field usually emphasizes engineering technology. It often assumes that you have taken the math courses listed above while in high school. It typically includes the other core courses listed above. It also includes those listed for the software emphasis, plus the following:

- Applied Differential Calculus
- Chemistry
- Data and File Structures
- Operating System Design

- Microcomputer-Based System Design
- Software Engineering
- Senior Design Project

Things to Know

You need good communications skills to succeed in this field. A writing course and probably a public speaking course, should be part of your programme even if they are not required.

Consider taking some business courses. Engineering technologists often work closely with management. In addition, the skills you learn in these courses may later help you make a career shift into management. This can be a logical and fulfilling career path, especially if you are uninterested in becoming a licensed engineer (or if your state does not allow it).

A lot of people are unclear about the difference among an engineer, an engineering technologist and an engineering technician. All work as part of an engineering team. Together, they solve practical problems by applying principles of science and math. The engineer tends to work more in theoretical terms and is more concerned with design. The engineering technologist tends to work more in practical terms and is more concerned with putting the design into practice. The technician gathers data and works with equipment to make the implementation work.

With a bachelor's degree in an engineering technology, you may be able to work either as an engineer or as a technologist. Your options depend on where you live. About one-third of the states do not allow engineering technology graduates to be licensed as engineers. Other states allow the license but restrict what you can do. Without a license, you still can have a rewarding job as part of the engineering team.

If you want a license and you are allowed by your state to seek one, you usually must have a bachelor's degree from an engineering technology programme recognized by the Accreditation Board for Engineering and Technology. (In this field, there are fewer than 20.) Then, you need several years of work experience and must pass an exam. Often you can take the exam in two stages. Your best bet is to take the first exam when you graduate or soon afterward.

Computer Installation and Repair

Computer installation and repair technology programmes prepare people to install, maintain and repair computers. Students learn how to programme and network computer systems. They learn about computer components such as power systems, chips and buffers.

It can be exciting to purchase a new computer. More memory, more RAM, better graphics, more bells and whistles! Yet it can also be intimidating to bring that big box home and try to set it up. You need to make sure that the monitor, CPU, keyboard and mouse all "talk" to each other the right way. And then there's the issue of setting up your Internet and e-mail access and getting connected to your printer. Sometimes, you think, it'd just be so much easier to pay someone else to do this for you!

What if you had to set up computers for a whole company? So many employees, so many computers! Not to mention the fact that each terminal must connect to the others so that files and information can be shared. And what if one computer breaks down? What happens if you need an important document that happened to be stored on that computer's hard drive?

Enter computer installation and repair technicians. These are the people who can help. They've studied how computers are put together and how to fix common computer problems. They aren't afraid of handling memory problems, error messages, or setting up your new personal digital assistant (PDA) so that it can upload files from your desktop. They understand how things connect and what phrases such as "network interface cards" and "computer architecture" mean.

In computer installation and repair programmes, you learn how to put together and take apart different kinds of computers. You also learn how to install, operate, maintain and repair them. You take courses about electronics, operating systems and programming. You also study computer networks, memory and peripheral equipment (*e.g.*, PDAs, printers). You learn how to fix common computer problems and how to interact with clients.

Computer installation and repair technology programmes are offered at about 25 community colleges, technical institutes, vocational centres and occasionally through high schools. They typically take from two months to a year to complete. In addition, some schools offer associate degrees in this field. These usually take one to two years to complete. However, most programmes are at the certificate level. As with many jobs, people with degrees in the field are usually able to advance to higher level positions.

With a background in computer installation and repair, you can work nearly anywhere that computers are used. You can work for large or small businesses as part of the team that handles the computer network. Many people start their own business or become independent contractors. This means that you work for hire."

College Preparation: For this programme, you should be comfortable using computers and the Internet. You should also be familiar with different operating systems.

You can prepare for this programme of study by completing your high school degree or getting a GED.

- General Computer Applications
- Computing Systems
- Computer Science and Programming
- Electricity
- Pre-Calculus

Typical Course Work

This programme typically includes courses in the following subjects:

- Advanced Configuration
- Computer Architecture
- Computer Hardware
- Computer Information Systems
- Computer Memory

- Computer Programming
- Computer Software
- Customer Relations
- Digital Electronics
- Network Management
- Operating Systems
- Peripheral Equipment
- Principles of Computer Repair
- World Wide Web and the Internet

Things to Know

Many computer support technicians decide to become certified. There are several different types of certification, but usually you must complete course work in computer installation and repair and have at least six months' work experience.

Computer Systems Networking

Programmes in computer systems networking and administration prepare people to manage linked systems of computers and devices. Students learn to design, implement and run these systems. They learn to evaluate security needs and develop safeguards. They also learn to manage computer usage.

When people think of the Internet, they often think of their favourite web site. Or, they think of it as a place to research and find information. But do you ever think about the fact that the Internet is one giant computer network? After all, the information and your favourite web sites have to come from somewhere. In fact, they're stored on servers all around the world. When you look up how to get to the Picasso museum in Barcelona, Spain, for example, your computer is connecting to another computer in another continent!

Network and systems administrators are people who manage computer networks and systems. They make sure that the links between computers, software, servers and printers and other equipment are working properly. They make sure that data is stored and backed up. They also make sure that information is kept secure. This includes keeping hackers out of sensitive files that include personal data. Overall, network and systems administrators want to keep the flow of information between computers smooth and safe and effortless for end users to the people who use the individual computers that are part of the larger network.

In computer systems networking and administration programmes, you study the basics to computer programming, operating systems and hardware and software. You also take courses about database management, security issues and ways to fix problems. Most importantly, you learn about different kinds of servers and networks. You learn about making networks run smoothly and efficiently. In addition, you study techniques for updating systems and storing data. You learn how to use computer equipment "off the shelf" as well as designing original software or equipment for different network and system needs.

Community colleges, technical colleges and vocational schools offer programmes ranging from one to two years. They are designed to prepare students for jobs as entry-level network or systems administrators. Many colleges and universities offer bachelor's degree programmes. Graduates of these programmes are prepared with a broad base of knowledge of the networks and servers that they can apply to business activities.

With a degree in computer systems networking and administration, you can be called many titles: systems administrator, network analyst, project manager, or probably the most common term: "the computer person."

Because new kinds of computers, servers and network systems are constantly developed or updated, many network and systems professionals choose to become specialized in addition to getting a degree in the field. Without specialized certification, it would be nearly impossible to keep up with all the changes in computer technology.

Specialized certificate programmes in computer systems networking are usually offered through community colleges, technical institutes, or vocational schools. Some programmes are offered through online courses or proprietary schools. These programmes vary in length from a few weeks to a year or more.

Common certifications are for Microsoft, Cisco, Nortel, Enterasys and Linux/UNIX networks and software. Keep in mind that you don't just become a Cisco certified administrator, for example. There are different types of certifications for each vendor. These certification programmes focus on different applications, from wireless networking to firewalls.

In general, your courses will concentrate on the specific computer networks and systems you wish to specialize in. You also study how to troubleshoot and debug network and system setups. This means that you learn how to test them for errors before they go live. You can concentrate on local area and wide area networks, or LANs and WANs. You can concentrate on Internet applications, such as e-commerce. Or, you can specialize in data security and storage.

In general, most two-year degrees can be transferred to four-year colleges and universities. In addition, graduate study is possible through programmes in computer science or management information systems. Check out these programmes of study for further information on a master's or doctorate degree."

College Preparation: For this programme, schools recommend that you know how to use a computer and the Internet.

You can prepare for this programme by taking courses in high school that prepare you for college. This typically includes four years of English, three years of math, three years of social studies and two years of science. Some colleges also require two years of a second language.

- Computing Systems
- Network Technology
- Computer Science and Programming
- Advanced Algebra courses
- Calculus

Undergraduate Special

For admission to specialized certification courses and programmes, you usually are required to have taken several courses in computer programming and general computer science. Depending on the certification you are seeking, you may need a degree in the field or networking experience.

Typical Course Work

This undergraduate programme typically includes courses in the following subjects:

- Computer and Network Security
- Computer Architecture
- Computer User Support
- Data and Computer Communications
- Database Administration
- Internet and World Wide Web
- Introduction to Computer and Network Administration
- Local Area Networks (LAN)
- Network and Systems Repair
- Operating Systems
- Peripheral Installation
- Programming Languages
- System Analysis and Design
- Unix Programming
- Wide Area Networks (WAN)

Things to Know

It is common for employers to require you to have a bachelor's degree in computer network systems administration to gain entry-level work in the field.

Certificate programmes in computer network systems administration are often offered. These are usually for people who already have a bachelor's degree in a related field and have professional computer experience.

Computer Networking

The need for seamlessly moving information across the globe for many to use and share through computers and Internet has given birth to computer networking.

Networking is changing the world of consumer electronics, biomedicine, industrial automation, super computing and defence. With the advent of Ethernet-enabled sensors and controllers, companies are increasingly looking at hooking their factory floor to their executive offices and beyond. Enterprise management is another widespread application made possible by networking.

The Work: Computer network management is a purely technical function. In a world where connectivity is the key, expertise in networking can take you places. There are several career avenues within networking, some of which are the following: Instead of working in a bank, credit card company or telecom company where you get to interact face-to-face with the custom

Network Administration: Working from the concept upwards, network administration involves configuring and managing LANs (Local Area Networks), WANs (Wide Area Networks) and VPNs (Virtual Private Networks). You will be responsible for analysing, installing and configuring the company's network even from a remote location. Monitoring network performance, troubleshooting problems and maintaining network security has to be done on a daily basis. With the proliferation of B2C (business to customer) websites, e-commerce, e-governance, VPN (Virtual Private Networks) and other Internet and telecom-based applications like remote servicing and IVR (Interactive Voice Response) the demand for network administrators is expected to peak in the next couple of years.

Familiarity with the intricacies of the specific systems being used by a company: Windows NT, Novell, Unix, Linux and so forth, thorough knowledge of networked applications, security and virus-protection schemes, system diagnostic utilities and experience with routers, hubs and bridges is also necessary.

Network Technicians: Focus more on the set up, troubleshooting and repair of specific hardware and software products.

Service Technicians: Visit customer sites to perform "field" upgrades and support functions.

Network Programmers and Analysts: Write software programmes or scripts that help evaluate third party products and integrate new software technologies into an existing or new network environment.

Network Managers: Supervise the work of administrators, engineers, technicians and programmers. They also work at long-range planning and strategy. At the entry level you will be focusing on tasks such as troubleshooting, monitoring, LAN performance, adding or deleting users, adding new servers, etc.

Network Security: As more and more organisations move their offline transactions online and vast quantities of vital and sensitive data travels through networks, the need for developing "fool proof" e-security systems to safeguard the networks and databases from rampant cracking has emerged as the number one IT concern globally. And consequently, it is one of the hottest and most sought-after specialities.

With over 300 new viruses released everyday and rampant hacking (82,000 recorded cases, according to a Carnegie Mellon University study, governments and corporations have beefed-up their IS spend and tightened access to their systems and core applications. They are looking for people who can administer their enterprise network security safely and securely as a strategic priority.

To excel in this field, you must be as familiar with system programming and administration as with security configuration and firewalls. This also includes knowledge of advanced TCP/IP, security fundamentals, security implementation, router security and attack routes.

Employment Opportunities: The Indian market for computers and peripherals has been growing at a rapid pace. In fact, the networking market is one of the fastest growing segments in the industry. Over three million units were sold in FY 2003-04 and the figure is expected to grow by 40 per cent crossing the 4.2 million mark in 2004-05. Driving this boom are technological innovations and a drop in prices, thanks to the IT agreement under the WTO, which will soon come into effect (translating into a PC penetration of 20 per 1000). Going by the average requirement of one hardware engineer for every 50 machines, the demand for networking professionals is bound to increase.

Moreover, Internet usage is increasing by the day and correspondingly the need for larger bandwidth for simultaneous transfer of data, voice and visuals (still and streaming video). The spurt in demand, has in turn, spurred the need for next generation data services like broadband access, virtual private networking, Voice over Internet Protocol (VOIP) and hi-tech Video Conferencing. With the tremendous growth in telecommunications and networking, people with good knowledge of computer network management on various platforms are in high demand. No doubt then, that there's a considerable demand gap in the availability of networking professionals globally. Whereas over 1,00,000 networking technicians and engineers are required, there are barely 50,000 of them presently.

What it takes?: Knowledge of computer hardware is the foundation for a career in computer networking. A good course will familiarise you with the basics of operating systems, microprocessors, peripheral devices, computer architecture, assembly and disassembly, installing various software, configuring PCs, preventive maintenance and troubleshooting.

This can be followed by a relevant course/s or certification in networking to gain expertise in LAN and WAN, which is in high demand.

LAN shares the information and resources within the premises through the intranet with the help of products like Windows NT or Windows 2003 from Microsoft, Unix from SCO, Solaris from Sun Microsystems, Netware from Novell, etc. It can be further connected to the Internet through internet working devices such as Routers and Switches.

WAN is a combination of Internet and Intranet — a network of networks, as it were.

Vendor certifications like Microsoft's MCSE or Cisco's CCNA or CCNP or CCIE, or Novel's CNE or Sun Microsystems' Sun Solaris Administrator at the higher end, are increasingly sought by recruiters.

What you'll Make?: Entry level salaries can be as high as Rs.20,000–25,000 for those with relevant vendor certifications like CCNA, etc. Diploma holders could expect to earn Rs.7,000–10,000. At the higher end a CTO (Chief Technology Officer) would get Rs 40,000. Those with good knowledge of ISPs, TCP/IP and the three-odd protocols, lease lines, particularly Microsoft Exchange Server 2003, command anything between Rs.75,000 upto 1.5 lakh+ (plus hefty perks).

Where to Study?: The basic qualification for getting into networking is preferably a Degree/Diploma in Computer Sc/Electrical/Electronics/Telecommunication followed by a course in computer hardware.

People with non-engineering background who possess good knowledge of computer fundamentals can also enter this field.

In addition, recruiters prefer certain global certifications.

Some of the popular International Certifications available for LAN/WAN Administration are MCSE, UNIX Admin, LINUX Admin, CNE, etc., whereas for WAN Administration you need CCNA, CCNP, CCDA, CCDP, CCIE.

Internet Security is an emerging technology in networking, which can be implemented by using Firewalls. A large part of the firewall implementation worldwide is done by Checkpoint/Computer Associates.

However, the most preferred certification is VUE Prometric as it covers most certifications — irrespective of the vendor platform.

Coaching facilities for clearing the various online tests for certification are offered at a number of Authorised Training Centres (ATCs) of the company. You can clear the (somewhat tough) test within 6 months of gaining some practical hands-on experience at any hardware establishment specialising in system integration.

Computer, Automated Teller and Office Machine Repairers

Significant Points: Workers qualify for these jobs by receiving training in electronics from associate degree programmes, the military, vocational schools, equipment manufacturers, or employers.

Job growth reflects the increasing dependence of businesses and individuals on computers and other sophisticated office machines.

Job prospects will be best for applicants with knowledge of electronics as well as repair experience.

Nature of the Work: *Computer repairers*, also known as *computer service technicians or data processing equipment repairers,* service mainframe, server and personal computers; printers; and disc drives. These workers perform primarily hands-on repair, maintenance and installation of computers and related equipment. Workers who provide technical assistance, in person or by telephone, to computer system users are known as computer support specialists or computer support technicians.

Automated teller machines (ATMs) allow customers to carry out bank transactions without the assistance of a teller. ATMs now also provide a growing variety of other services, including stamp, phone card and ticket sales. *Automated teller machine servicers* repair and service these machines.

Office machine and cash register servicers work on photocopiers, cash registers, mail-processing equipment and fax machines. Newer models of office machinery include computerized components that allow them to function more effectively than earlier models.

To install large equipment, such as mainframe computers and ATMs, repairers connect the equipment to power sources and communication lines that allow the transmission of information over computer networks. For example, when an ATM dispenses cash, it transmits the withdrawal information to the customer's bank. Workers also may install operating software and peripheral equipment, checking that all components are configured to function together correctly. The installation of personal computers and other small office machines is less complex and may be handled by the purchaser.

When equipment breaks down, many repairers travel to customers' workplaces or other locations to make the necessary repairs. These workers, known as *field technicians*, often have assigned areas in which they perform preventive maintenance on a regular basis. *Bench technicians* work in repair shops located in stores, factories, or service centres. In small companies, repairers may work both in repair shops and at customer locations.

Computer repairers usually replace subsystems instead of repairing them. Replacement is common because subsystems are inexpensive and businesses are reluctant to shut down their computers for time-consuming repairs. Subsystems commonly replaced by computer repairers include video cards, which transmit signals from the computer to the monitor; hard drives, which store data; and network cards, which allow communication over the network. Defective modules may be given to bench technicians, who use software programmes to diagnose the problem and who may repair the modules, if possible.

When ATMs malfunction, computer networks recognize the problem and alert repairers. Common problems include worn magnetic heads on card readers, which prevent the equipment from recognizing customers' bankcards and "pick failures," which prevent the equipment from dispensing the correct amount of cash. Field technicians travel to the locations of ATMs and usually repair equipment by removing and replacing defective components. Broken components are taken to a repair shop, where bench technicians make the necessary repairs. Field technicians perform routine maintenance on a regular basis, replacing worn parts and running diagnostic tests to ensure that the equipment functions properly.

Office machine repairers usually work on machinery at the customer's workplace; alternatively, if the machines are small enough, customers may bring them to a repair shop for maintenance. Common malfunctions include paper misfeeds caused by worn or dirty parts and poor-quality copy resulting from problems with lamps, lenses, or mirrors. These malfunctions usually can be resolved simply by cleaning the relevant components. Breakdowns also may result from the failure of commonly used parts. For example, heavy use of a photocopier may wear down the printhead, which applies ink to the final copy. In such cases, the repairer usually replaces the part instead of repairing it.

Workers use a variety of tools for diagnostic tests and repair. To diagnose malfunctions, they use multimeters to measure voltage, current, resistance and other electrical properties; signal generators to provide test signals; and oscilloscopes to monitor equipment signals. To diagnose computerized equipment, repairers use software programmes. To repair or adjust equipment, workers use handtools, such as pliers, screwdrivers, soldering irons and wrenches.

Working Conditions: Repairers usually work in clean, well-lighted surroundings. Because computers and office machines are sensitive to extreme temperatures and to humidity, repair shops usually are air-conditioned and well ventilated. Field repairers must travel frequently to various locations to install, maintain, or repair customers' equipment. ATM repairers may have to perform their jobs in small, confined spaces that house the equipment.

Because computers and ATMs are critical for many organizations to function efficiently, data processing equipment repairers and ATM field technicians often work around the clock. Their schedules may include evening, weekend and holiday shifts, sometimes assigned on the basis of seniority. Office machine and cash register servicers usually work regular business hours because the equipment they repair is not as critical.

Although their job is not strenuous, repairers must lift equipment and work in a variety of postures. Repairers of computer monitors need to discharge voltage from the equipment to avoid electrocution. Workers may have to wear protective goggles.

Training, Other Qualifications and Advancement: Knowledge of electronics is necessary for employment as a computer, automated teller, or office machine repairer. Employers prefer workers who are certified as repairers or who have training in electronics from associate degree programmes, the military, vocational schools, or equipment manufacturers. Employers generally provide some training to new repairers on specific equipment; however, workers are expected to arrive on the job with a basic understanding of equipment repair. Employers may send experienced workers to training sessions to keep up with changes in technology and service procedures.

Most office machine and ATM repairer positions require an associate degree in electronics. A basic understanding of mechanical equipment also is important, because many of the parts that fail in office machines and ATMs, such as paper loaders, are mechanical. Entry-level employees at large companies normally receive on-the-job training lasting several months. Such training may include a week of classroom instruction, followed by a period of 2 weeks to several months assisting an experienced repairer.

Field technicians work closely with customers and must have good communications skills and a neat appearance. Employers normally require that field technicians have a driver's license.

Various organizations offer certification. To receive certification, repairers must pass qualifying examinations corresponding to their level of training and experience.

Newly hired computer repairers may work on personal computers or peripheral equipment. With experience, they can advance to positions maintaining more sophisticated systems, such as networking equipment and servers. Field repairers of ATMs may advance to bench technician positions responsible for more complex repairs. Experienced workers may become specialists who help other repairers diagnose difficult problems or who work with engineers in designing equipment and developing maintenance procedures. Experienced workers also may move into management positions responsible for supervising other repairers.

Because of their familiarity with equipment, experienced repairers may move into customer service or sales positions. Some experienced workers open their own repair shops or become wholesalers or retailers of electronic equipment.

Employment: Computer, automated teller and office machine repairers held about 168,000 jobs in 2004. Wholesale trade establishments employed about 35 percent of the workers in this occupation; most of these establishments were wholesalers of professional and commercial equipment and supplies. Many workers also were employed in electronics, appliance and office supply stores. Others worked in electronic and precision equipment repair shops and computer systems design firms. A small number found employment with computer and peripheral equipment manufacturers, government agencies and Internet service providers. About 15 percent of computer, automated teller and office machine repairers were self-employed, which is more than twice the proportion for all installation, maintenance and repair occupations.

Job Outlook: Employment of computer, automated teller and office machine repairers is expected to grow **more slowly than the average** for all occupations through 2014. Limited job growth will be driven by the increasing dependence of business and individuals on computers and other sophisticated office machines. The need to maintain this equipment will create new jobs for repairers. In addition, openings will result from the need to replace repairers who retire or transfer to new occupations.

Job prospects will be best for applicants with knowledge of electronics as well as repair experience. Although computer equipment continues to become less expensive and more reliable, malfunctions still occur and can cause severe problems for users, most of whom lack the knowledge to make repairs. Computers are critical to most businesses today and will become even more so to companies that do business on the Internet and to individuals that bank, pay bills, or make purchases online.

People also are becoming increasingly reliant on ATMs. Besides offering bank and retail transactions, ATMs provide an increasing number of other services, such as employee information processing and distribution of government payments. Improvements in ATM design have increased reliability and simplified repair tasks, reducing the number and extent of repairs. However, opportunities for ATM repairers should still be available arising primarily from the need to replace workers who leave the specialty, rather than from employment growth.

Conventional office machines, such as calculators, are inexpensive and often are replaced instead of repaired. However, digital copiers and other, newer office machines are more costly and complex. This equipment often is computerized, designed to work on a network and capable of performing multiple functions. The growing need for repairers to service such sophisticated equipment should result in job opportunities for office machine repairers.

Earnings: Median hourly earnings of computer, automated teller and office machine repairers were $16.90 in May 2004. The middle 50 percent earned between $13.11 and $21.36. The lowest 10 percent earned less than $10.31 and the highest 10 percent earned more than $26.28. Median hourly earnings in the industries employing the largest numbers of computer, automated teller and office machine repairers in May 2004 are shown below:

Professional and commercial equipment and supplies merchant wholesalers	$18.51
Computer systems design and related services	18.08
Office supplies, stationery and gift stores	15.69
Electronic and precision equipment repair and maintenance	14.95
Electronics and appliance stores	14.04

Assembly Technician

Computer assembly technicians build computers from their parts, such as circuit boards, disk drives, cables and switches. When they have put the parts together, they test the computer and correct any faults.

Work Activities: Computer assembly technicians build complete computers from their parts. For an ordinary PC (personal computer), these would include:

- external case

- power supply unit
- disk drives
- processor
- circuit boards
- cooling fan
- cables and switches.

Computer assembly technicians gather the necessary items from stockrooms and warehouses as required. They fit the parts and wire them up, then test that the finished computer is working correctly. If it is not, they perform a series of further tests to discover where the fault lies and correct the fault.

Technicians working for a computer manufacturer typically assemble a series of machines with identical specifications. If they work for a smaller specialist supplier or retailer, they may construct each machine according to a different set of specifications as required by the customer. In such cases, assembly technicians may also become involved in dealing with customers and perhaps servicing and upgrading existing machines.

They use tools such as screwdrivers and soldering irons and electronic testing equipment such as multimeters and oscilloscopes. Some of the components used in computers are quite delicate and sensitive, so they may have to wear special outer clothing to reduce the risk of contamination by dust or dirt. Also, static electricity can damage some circuit boards, so they may have to avoid wearing certain items (for example, man-made fabrics such as nylon) which can allow static to build up. They may also have to wear anti-static wristbands and other static-reducing items.

Personal Qualities and Skills: As a computer assembly technician, you will need an interest in computers and electronics. You will also need good manual dexterity, as many of the parts are small and delicate. You must also be able to work reasonably quickly.

You will need a methodical approach and the ability to follow written instructions precisely. You will also have to be conscientious and careful, as mistakes made during assembly can be costly and time-consuming to put right later. When a newly-built machine fails to work properly, you may need patience and perseverance to identify the source of the problem and fix it.

A reasonable level of physical fitness/stamina is desirable, as computer assembly technicians spend much of their day performing repetitive manual tasks such as soldering and inserting circuit boards. You may also have to carry heavy computers or computer components to and from stockrooms and workshops.

Pay and Opportunities: The pay rates given below are approximate. Computer assembly technicians earn £200—£230 a week, rising to £290—£350 a week. Higher earners can make around £400 a week.

Assembly technicians typically work 39 hours, Monday to Friday. Shift work and early morning starts may be required. Part-time work and overtime may be available.

Employers include large computer manufacturers and firms that supply electronic parts and assemblies to them.

The following information is sourced from government statistics. The government's definition of types of job is slightly different to that used in this programme. For this type of job, the most relevant government-defined occupation is 'Assemblers (electrical products)'.

In 2001 there were 3,600 people working as 'Assemblers (electrical products)' in Scotland. 16 in every 10,000 employees working in Scotland were employed as 'Assemblers (electrical products)'.

Estimates of projected future job openings requiring new entrants to the jobs market are available, but not at the level of detail of 'Assemblers (electrical products)'. Employment levels for the broader occupational type of 'Assemblers and Routine Operatives' are projected to decline over the five years between 2003 and 2008 and there will be limited job opportunities for new employees.

3 out of every 20 employees work part time in this type of job.

Entry Routes and Training: New entrants may be able to train through a Skillseekers/Modern Apprenticeship. This combines on-the-job training with off-the-job training at a college or training centre and leads to SVQ levels 2/3.

Qualifications: There is no minimum entry requirement for this occupation. Applicants may have to perform an aptitude test to check whether they have the skills and dexterity needed for this career.

According to government statistics, employees in this type of job have the following qualifications. Higher Education: Fewer than one in ten employees have their highest level of qualifications attained at degree level or equivalent or higher. Post-16 or Further Education: 2 out of 10 employees have their highest qualification at a level below a degree or higher degree or equivalent, but gained after the age of 16. School leaving age (16) qualifications or qualifications at SVQ3: 7 out of 10 employees gained their highest qualification at the age of 16 or have gained another qualification lower than a VQ level 3 since they were 16.

Computer Games Designer

Computer games designers devise the concept for computer games and help determine the way they look and play. They begin with an outline of the game and use a variety of tools to produce a final script for the game.

Work Activities: Computer games have become a familiar aspect of life in modern Britain. Computer games designers are the people who dream up these games and help determine the way they look and play.

Games are developed for a number of different 'platforms' (types of computer). The most important are PCs (personal computers) and consoles (dedicated games machines). A growing number of games are now also played online via the Internet.

Computer games designers devise the basic concepts for these games. The original inspiration may be a book, film or short story, or it may come entirely from the designer's own imagination.

Typically, they begin with an outline that sets out the story of the game in linear form. However, because computer games are interactive (the player's actions play a crucial part in determining how the story unfolds), they develop from this a complex script showing all the options a player might take and the consequences, leading to one or more different conclusions. To do this, they use tools such as flowcharts, storyboards and index cards. Many of these tools are available in the form of computer programmes. Eventually, perhaps working with one or more writers, they produce a final script for the entire game.

In association with the art director, computer game designers are also responsible for the overall look of a game. To this end, they may produce sketches and storyboards and design the 'interface', which is what a player sees while actually playing the game. The interface is a crucial part of any game design, because it determines how it feels to play the game and the kind of choices that a player has available at any time.

Games designers also increasingly use 'level editors' which provide a user-friendly interface between 'old-fashioned' coding and a standard graphic design programme. Level editors are used for building up a game's 2D or 3D world. Level editors often come packaged with the game at retail, allowing players to design their own levels for games. This can be a good way for aspiring designers to improve their skills and build up a portfolio of work.

Computer game designers work in a tightly-knit team, which also includes graphic artists, writers, musicians and programmers. The team is led by a project manager. In practice, many team members will have a range of skills and the industry is full of writer-designers, artist-programmers, designer-producers and so on. Different designers have different skills and strengths, some leaning more towards the writing, others more towards visual aspects of the design.

Personal Qualities and Skills: As a computer games designer, you will need an interest in computers and a good knowledge of (and enthusiasm for) computer games.

You will require a strong visual imagination and the ability to work with highly complex, multi-stranded scripts and programmes. A logical, methodical approach is therefore essential. You will also need to be patient and painstaking, as developing a new game from scratch is a lengthy and demanding process.

You will need to be a good team worker. Artistic/design skills are essential and for some types of computer game, script-writing skills are also important. Some programming knowledge/ability is desirable. However, computer games designers do not necessarily have to be expert computer programmers.

Pay and Opportunities: The pay rates given below are approximate. Salaries for computer games designers are in the range of £19,500—£25,500 a year, rising to £38,000. Higher earners can make around £49,500 a year. Salaries may include performance-related pay, profit sharing or company bonuses.

Games designers usually work a basic 37-hour week, Monday to Friday. However, late finishes and weekend work may be required, especially as deadlines approach. Self-employed designers may work longer and more irregular hours.

The UK has a small but thriving computer games industry and skilled personnel are much in demand. There are also good opportunities to work in France, the USA and Japan, where many more computer games companies are based. Employers range from large firms involved in creating, publishing and marketing new games, to smaller software publishing houses that specialise in a particular range of games.

Vacancies are published in the national press and also in specialist magazines such as 'Edge' and 'Computer Trade Weekly', both of which have online internet recruitment sections.

Some designers are employed on a short-term or fixed-term contract basis.

The following information is sourced from government statistics. The government's definition of types of job is slightly different to that used in this programme. For this type of job, the most relevant Government-defined occupation is 'Software professionals'.

In 2001 there were 17,200 people working as 'Software professionals' in Scotland. 80 in every 10,000 employees working in Scotland were employed as 'Software professionals'.

Estimates of projected future job openings requiring new entrants to the jobs market are available, but not at the level of detail of 'Software professionals'. It is estimated that over the five years between 2003 and 2008 there will be a need for 7,000 new employees to fill vacancies in the broader occupational type of 'Information & Communication Technology'.

1 out of every 20 employees works part time in this type of job.

Entry Routes and Training: While there are no formal entry qualifications, some hold a degree or Higher National qualification in computer-related subjects, such as computer science, computer visualisation and animation, digital arts or computer graphics. Others are graduates of art and design courses.

Mature entrants need relevant skills and experience to enter the industry.

Qualifications: There are no formal minimum requirements for entry to this work. Applicants with an interest in computer game design, coupled with a good imagination and plenty of fresh ideas, can be as successful as those who hold formal qualifications such as a Higher National Diploma or a degree in graphic design.

For entry to a degree course the minimum requirement is 3 Highers (A-C) plus Standard Grades (1-3) in 2 other subjects.

However, entry requirements vary between courses and alternative qualifications may be accepted—check prospectuses for details.

According to government statistics, employees in this type of job have the following qualifications. Higher Education: 7 out of 10 employees have their highest level of qualifications attained at degree level or equivalent or higher. Post-16 or Further Education: 2 out of 10 employees have their highest qualification at a level below a degree or higher degree or equivalent, but gained after the age of 16. School leaving age (16) qualifications or qualifications at SVQ3: 2 out of 10 employees gained their highest qualification at the age of 16 or have gained another qualification lower than a VQ level 3 since they were 16.

Computer Games Programmer

Computer games programmers turn the ideas of games designers into games that people can actually play. They do this by writing computer code or using a range of programming tools that generate code for them.

Work Activities: Computer games programmers develop games for a number of different 'platforms' (types of computer). The most important are PCs (personal computers) and consoles (dedicated games machines). A growing number of games are also now played online via the Internet.

Computer games programmers work as members of a tightly-knit production team, which normally also includes designers, writers, musicians and graphic artists. The team is led by a project manager. The programmer provides the technical expertise to turn the ideas of the designer, writer and other production team members into reality on the computer screen.

To do this, programmers either write the code in an appropriate computer language such as C/C++, Java or Pascal, or they use a range of special programming tools that generate the actual code for them.

Modern computer games are extremely complex, so there is usually a team of programmers working on each one. The actual programming is divided into a number of tasks, with each one assigned to a different programmer. This requires efficient teamwork and co-ordination and special CASE (computer-assisted software engineering) tools are often used to ensure consistency is achieved and that programmers are not duplicating each other's work.

Once the coding is complete, the programmer tests the application to make sure that it works correctly and there are no faults. This 'de-bugging' can prove a time-consuming process, though most programming applications include special software tools to assist in the process.

Personal Qualities and Skills: As a computer games programmer, you will need an interest in computers and a good knowledge of (and enthusiasm for) computer games. Advanced programming skills, preferably in a number of different computer languages, are essential.

As with most computer-related jobs, you will require a logical, methodical approach to your work. You will also need to be patient and painstaking, as developing a new game from scratch is a long and demanding process.

You will need to be a good team worker, able to get along with others and meet deadlines. You must also be willing to spend many hours sitting at a computer developing code. Good problem-solving abilities are essential when attempting to remove 'bugs' and to find ways to solve complex programming challenges.

Pay and Opportunities: Salaries for computer games programmers vary depending on the range of their responsibilities and the size and type of company they work for. The pay rates given below are approximate. Salaries are in the range of £19,500—£25,500 a year, rising to £38,000. Higher earners can make around £49,500 a year. Salaries may include performance-related pay, profit sharing or company bonuses.

Computer games programmers usually work 35—37 hours, Monday to Friday. However, late finishes and some weekend work are often required, especially as deadlines approach.

The UK has a small but thriving computer games industry and skilled personnel are much in demand. There are also good opportunities to work in France, the USA and Japan, where many more computer games companies are based.

Employers range from large firms involved in creating, publishing and marketing new games, to smaller software publishing houses that specialise in a particular range of games. Self-employment is possible for experienced programmers. Short-term contract work can be available through specialist IT recruitment agencies.

The following information is sourced from government statistics. The government's definition of types of job is slightly different to that used in this programme. For this type of job, the most relevant Government-defined occupation is 'Software professionals'.

In 2001 there were 17,200 people working as 'Software professionals' in Scotland. 80 in every 10,000 employees working in Scotland were employed as 'Software professionals'.

Estimates of projected future job openings requiring new entrants to the jobs market are available, but not at the level of detail of 'Software professionals'. It is estimated that over the five years between 2003 and 2008 there will be a need for 7,000 new employees to fill vacancies in the broader occupational type of 'Information & Communication Technology'.

1 out of every 20 employees works part time in this type of job.

Entry Routes and Training: There are no formal minimum entry requirements for this occupation, though in practice most programmers possess at least one or two Highers or a relevant vocational qualification. A growing number possess a degree or Higher National Diploma in a computing subject.

More important than formal qualifications in this field is the possession of relevant skills and/or experience.

Qualifications: For entry to a degree course the minimum requirement is 3 Highers (A-C) plus Standard Grades (1-3) in 2 other subjects.

Other relevant qualifications at National Certificate, Higher National Certificate or Higher National Diploma level may also be considered. However, it may be possible to enter this work with no formal qualifications if you have relevant skills and/ or experience.

According to government statistics, employees in this type of job have the following qualifications. Higher Education: 7 out of 10 employees have their highest level of qualifications attained at degree level or equivalent or higher. Post-16 or Further Education: 2 out of 10 employees have their highest qualification at a level below a degree or higher degree or equivalent, but gained after the age of 16. School leaving age (16) qualifications or qualifications at SVQ3: 2 out of 10 employees gained their highest qualification at the age of 16 or have gained another qualification lower than a VQ level 3 since they were 16.

Computer Hardware Engineer

Computer hardware engineers work on the design, development and manufacture of computer hardware. They may specialise in areas such as communications, control systems, robotics, microprocessors or semi-conductor devices.

Work Activities: Some hardware engineers research and design very advanced and sophisticated technology. For example, hardware engineers are working on using different wavelengths of light on one optical fibre to increase the amount of data that can be transmitted at once.

Engineers make most computers by buying microprocessing chips, assembling components and equipment and linking them up together to form a system. The process may begin with the computer systems analyst providing an outline specification for a computer system to meet a particular need. A team of logic designers works on the initial logic design and produces detailed specifications. They translate the ideas into detailed drawings and circuit diagrams.

A team of hardware engineers takes the design and builds and tests a prototype or working model. They buy the computer chips, assemble the hardware components and build the necessary interfacing equipment. They test the prototype to make sure it meets the specification requirements; they carry out any necessary modifications to the design.

Personal Qualities and Skills: To be a computer hardware engineer, you need strong technical knowledge of computers and electronic systems. You must have a flair for turning system requirements into detailed designs. You need to be able to work to deadlines and budgets; you may also need to consider the cost and availability of components. Computer hardware engineers must be able to work as part of multi-disciplinary teams; you must have strong oral and written communication skills.

Pay and Opportunities: Salaries for engineers vary. The pay rates given below are approximate. Computer hardware engineers earn £21,000—£25,000 a year, rising to £29,500—£36,500 . Higher earners can make around £47,000 a year.

Hardware engineers usually work up to 37 hours, Monday to Friday.

Employers are computer manufacturers, electronics companies, retailers and distributors of computers, information technology consultants and software or systems houses.

The following information is sourced from government statistics. The government's definition of types of job is slightly different to that used in this programme. For this type of job, the most relevant government-defined occupation is 'Software professionals'.

In 2001 there were 17,200 people working as 'Software professionals' in Scotland. 80 in every 10,000 employees working in Scotland were employed as 'Software professionals'.

Estimates of projected future job openings requiring new entrants to the jobs market are available, but not at the level of detail of 'Software professionals'. It is estimated that over the five years between 2003 and 2008 there will be a need for 7,000 new employees to fill vacancies in the broader occupational type of 'Information & Communication Technology'.

1 out of every 20 employees works part time in this type of job.

Entry Routes and Training: Computer hardware engineers normally complete an appropriate degree. Relevant course titles include Electronic and Computer Engineering and Computer Systems Engineering. It is essential to consult prospectuses to make sure the course you choose is appropriate to the branch of engineering you want to follow.

Computer hardware engineers can gain Chartered Engineer and Incorporated Engineer status, which are both highly regarded by employers throughout industry.

To register with the Engineering Council (UK) as a Chartered Engineer (CEng) or Incorporated Engineer (IEng), you must apply through an appropriate engineering professional institution.

To register as a Chartered Engineer, the usual route is to complete first an accredited degree, as listed on the Engineering Council (UK) website, *e.g.*. an M.Eng.

To register as an Incorporated Engineer, the usual route is to complete first an accredited degree, as listed on the Engineering Council (UK) website, *e.g.* a B.Eng.

After gaining your degree, you will undergo Initial Professional Development (IPD). This involves accredited training and responsible experience in the workplace. This is followed by a Professional Review with interview to assess your competence and commitment to Continued Professional Development (CPD).

Qualifications: The usual qualification for entry into this career is a degree. However, it is possible to enter through completion of a Higher National Diploma or Higher National Certificate.

The usual entry requirements for a degree in Computer Engineering are 3/5 Highers (A-C). Higher Maths is often essential and Physics or Computing may also be recommended.

The usual entry requirements for an HNC/HND are 1/3 Highers and Standard Grades.

However, entry qualifications vary between courses and alternative qualifications may be accepted—check prospectuses for details.

According to government statistics, employees in this type of job have the following qualifications. Higher Education: 7 out of 10 employees have their highest level of qualifications attained at degree level or equivalent or higher. Post-16 or Further Education: 2 out of 10 employees have their highest qualification at a level below a degree or higher degree or equivalent, but gained after the age of 16. School leaving age (16) qualifications or qualifications at SVQ3: 2 out of 10 employees gained their highest qualification at the age of 16 or have gained another qualification lower than a VQ level 3 since they were 16.

Helpline Operator: Computer helpline operators deal with telephone calls from people who are having computer problems. They find out what the problem is and then try to find a solution for the caller. They work for manufacturers of hardware and software, Internet service providers and large organisations whose staff use computers in their work.

Work Activities: Computer helpline operators help people overcome problems they may have while using a computer. Such problems may be related to the computer itself, but more often concern one or more specific applications. The latter might include:

- accounting programmes
- databases
- spreadsheets
- word processing programmes
- desktop publishing programmes
- computer-aided design (CAD) programmes
- computer games
- Internet-related software

Their work requires them to have an in-depth knowledge of the machines and/or applications enquirers are using. This is normally gained through a combination of on-the-job and off-the-job training, plus in many cases direct personal experience of working with the applications concerned.

Helpline operators work on 'help desks', taking telephone enquiries from users while wearing hands-free headsets. They first establish the nature and cause of users' problems and then talk them through the steps necessary to solve them. They have a computer in front of them from which they are able to obtain information and perhaps reproduce users' problems.

In some cases, problems may be due to mistakes made by the user, but in others they may be caused by a fault in the user's computer or the software. In such cases operators may have to advise users to return the item concerned to the supplier for a repair or refund.

Computer helpline operators work for a variety of institutions, including computer manufacturers/retailers, Internet access providers and software suppliers. They are also employed by some large organisations to provide help for staff who have to use computers in the course of their work.

Personal Qualities and Skills: As a computer helpline operator, you will need an interest in computers and a good knowledge of the applications concerned (though training will normally be provided). You will require a logical, methodical approach, as identifying the cause of a problem sometimes requires a certain amount of detective work.

Good communication skills and patience are important and you will need a calm, clear telephone manner.

Pay and Opportunities: Salaries for computer helpline operators vary depending on the size and type of company they work for and the level of technical competence required for the job. The pay rates given below are approximate. Helpline operators earn in the range of £16,000—£18,000 a year, rising to £23,500—£29,500. Higher earners can make around £36,000 a year. Salaries may include performance-related pay, profit sharing or company bonuses.

Computer helpline operators work a basic 35-hour week, Monday to Friday. Early starts, late finishes, weekend work and shift work may be required.

Employers, throughout the UK include computer manufacturers, software suppliers and Internet service providers. Firms in industry and commerce, including banks, building societies and insurance companies and those in the public sector; local and central government departments, the NHS and public utilities.

The following information is sourced from government statistics. The government's definition of types of job is slightly different to that used in this programme. For this type of job, the most relevant Government-defined occupation is 'IT user support technicians'.

In 2001 there were 4,000 people working as 'IT user support technicians' in Scotland. 18 in every 10,000 employees working in Scotland were employed as 'IT user support technicians'.

Estimates of projected future job openings requiring new entrants to the jobs market are available, but not at the level of detail of 'IT user support technicians'. It is estimated that over the five years between 2003 and 2008 there will be a need for 6,000 new employees to fill vacancies in the broader occupational type of 'IT Service Delivery Occupations'. 2 out of every 20 employees work part time in this type of job.

Entry Routes and Training: Most computer helpline operators have at least 4 or 5 Standard Grades (1-3) including Maths and English.

Many entrants train through a Skillseekers/Modern Apprenticeship. This combines on-the-job training with off-the-job training at a college or training centre and leads to SVQ levels 2/3.

It may be possible to work towards SVQs in Information Technology subjects at levels 2/3.

Qualifications: There are no minimum qualifications for entry to this work. However, employers are likely to ask for some Standard Grades (1-3) including English and Maths. Many entrants have at least 4 or 5 Standard Grades at 1-3.

It is not uncommon for people with higher qualifications, such as Highers and National Certificate/Higher National Certificate/Higher National Diploma qualifications to enter this work.

According to government statistics, employees in this type of job have the following qualifications. Higher Education: 5 out of 10 employees have their highest level of qualifications attained at degree level or equivalent or higher. Post-16 or Further Education: 2 out of 10 employees have their highest qualification at a level below a degree or higher degree or equivalent, but gained after the age of 16. School leaving age (16) qualifications or qualifications at SVQ3: 3 out of 10 employees gained their highest qualification at the age of 16 or have gained another qualification lower than a VQ level 3 since they were 16.

Computer Operator

Computer operators control the processing of work through large, mainframe computers. They load discs or tapes and run programmes. Operators take action when faults occur.

Work Activities: Computer operators control the processing of work through a mainframe computer. This is a large computer that is responsible for the central processing of an organisation's data. Usually, organisations that have to process a large volume of data use mainframe computers, for example, banks, local authorities, the Inland Revenue and the police.

Operators start up the mainframe computer (unless it runs constantly). Then they load data and programmes from magnetic tapes or discs and start up the process operation.

They control and check operations from a console, using a keyboard to type instructions to the computer and its peripheral (related) equipment. Older computer systems need the operator to type in commands at several stages. Modern systems are more automated. The operator may need only to load a special operations programme or type in an initial set of instructions for the computer to run a whole sequence of operations.

Operators have to check that the system, including the peripheral equipment, is working smoothly. For example, they must check that the printer is producing good quality printouts. If a fault occurs, operators have to find the problem. If the fault is with the hardware (the computer itself), they may have to carry out simple repairs. The operator has to make sure all data is saved on storage discs (or 'backed up') in case the system goes down.

This work also includes routine maintenance tasks such as checking the temperature and humidity in the room (mainframe computers need a carefully controlled environment). Operators run housekeeping programmes and clean equipment. They monitor how well the system works, keeping records to make sure the computer processes data as efficiently as possible.

Many organisations have replaced the mainframe computer with a system that allows individual computers to process data. This has significantly reduced the number of opportunities for computer operators.

Personal Qualities and Skills: As a computer operator, you will need strong technical knowledge. You must be able to work logically and methodically. You will also need the patience to make routine checks on the system. You must be able to cope well with pressure, for example, if the mainframe computer goes down. This means you need initiative, an analytical mind and good problem solving skills.

You should also have good communication skills to explain problems clearly and concisely to people who are not computer experts.

Pay and Opportunities: Salaries for computer operators vary depending on the range of their responsibilities and the size and type of company they work for. The pay rates given below are approximate. Salaries are in the range of £11,000—£12,500 a year, rising to £15,000—£21,500 a year. Higher earners can make around £29,000 a year.

Computer operators usually work 35—37 hours, Monday to Friday. Shift work, including weekend work on a rota basis, is common.

Employers, throughout the UK, are organisations that use a mainframe computer system, for example, local authorities, the Inland Revenue and the police and those in industry and commerce, such as oil companies, banks, building societies and insurance companies. Since one mainframe computer department can service an entire company's needs, staffing levels tend to be small.

The following information is sourced from government statistics. The government's definition of types of job is slightly different to that used in this programme. For this type of job, the most relevant Government-defined occupation is 'IT operations technicians'.

In 2001 there were 7,500 people working as 'IT operations technicians' in Scotland. 35 in every 10,000 employees working in Scotland were employed as 'IT operations technicians'.

Estimates of projected future job openings requiring new entrants to the jobs market are available, but not at the level of detail of 'IT operations technicians'. It is estimated that over the five years between 2003 and 2008 there will be a need for 6,000 new employees to fill vacancies in the broader occupational type of 'IT Service Delivery Occupations'.

2 out of every 20 employees work part time in this type of job.

Entry Routes and Training: New entrants may be able to train through a Skillseekers/Modern Apprenticeship. This combines on-the-job training with off-the-job training at a college or training centre and leads to SVQ levels 2/3.

A National Certificate/Qualification course in Computing/ Information Technology is an alternative starting point. Some employers may ask for Highers.

Qualifications: Entry requirements vary. It may be possible to enter this job with no formal qualifications and receive on-the-job training. Some employers ask for some Standard Grades or qualifications such as a National Certificate/ Qualification course in Computing/Information Technology.

According to government statistics, employees in this type of job have the following qualifications. Higher Education: 5 out of 10 employees have their highest level of qualifications attained at degree level or equivalent or higher. Post-16 or Further Education: 2 out of 10 employees have their highest qualification at a level below a degree or higher degree or equivalent, but gained after the age of 16. School leaving age (16) qualifications or qualifications at SVQ3: 3 out of 10 employees gained their highest qualification at the age of 16 or have gained another qualification lower than a VQ level 3 since they were 16.

Computer Service Technician

Computer service technicians maintain, update and service computer equipment and software in the organisations where they work or in third party organisations.

Work Activities: When new computers arrive from suppliers, computer service technicians check that they are as ordered, then connect and test them to make sure that they are working properly. They install any specialist software which the user may need (such as computer-aided design or e-mail programmes). They may also install the equipment at the user's workstation and perhaps provide basic instruction on how to use it.

Technicians also repair and upgrade older machines. This might involve such tasks as:

- installing extra RAM (memory)
- fitting a new hard disk
- repairing a faulty monitor
- connecting a new soundcard
- fitting a CD-ROM or DVD drive
- installing extra equipment, such as a scanner.

They may also work on other computer-related equipment, such as printers, scanners and digital cameras.

Where computer networks are used in the organisation, technicians may be responsible for administrative tasks such as issuing passwords and performing a daily backup, as well as dealing with any problems that crop up. If their main task involves supporting computer networks, they are likely to be given the job title network technician or network administrator.

Many computer service technicians are 'on call' for part or all of their working time to support users who have problems. This might involve explaining how a particular programme function works, or identifying and eradicating a computer virus. In some cases, computer service technicians may be able to talk users through their problem on the phone, but in others they may need to visit them personally. Where they cannot solve a particular problem, technicians may need to talk to suppliers and manufacturers' support staff to try to find a solution.

Personal Qualities and Skills: As a computer service technician, you will need an interest in computers and a logical, methodical approach to your work. Patience and perseverance are important. You will also need a good understanding of the hardware and software used in the organisation (though training is likely to be provided).

Good communication skills are important when speaking to users or clients. Some may not be able to explain their problem clearly, so you will need to be patient, asking questions to help clarify the nature of the problem, then suggesting steps they can take to overcome it.

A reasonable level of physical fitness/stamina is desirable, as computer service technicians may have to carry computers and other heavy equipment to and from storerooms and to users' offices. For some jobs, you may need a driving licence.

Pay and Opportunities: Salaries for computer services technicians vary, depending on the size and type of company they work for. The pay rates given below are approximate. Computer service technicians earn in the range of £14,500—£17,500 a year, rising to £22,500—£27,500. Higher earners can make around £35,500 a year.

Computer services technicians usually work a 37-hour week, Monday to Friday. Late finishes, on-call and weekend work may be required from time to time.

Employers throughout the UK are firms in industry and commerce, including banks, building societies and insurance companies and in the public sector with local and central government departments, the NHS and public utilities.

The following information is sourced from government statistics. The government's definition of types of job is slightly different to that used in this programme. For this type of job, the most relevant government-defined occupation is 'IT operations technicians'.

In 2001 there were 7,500 people working as 'IT operations technicians' in Scotland. 35 in every 10,000 employees working in Scotland were employed as 'IT operations technicians'.

Estimates of projected future job openings requiring new entrants to the jobs market are available, but not at the level of detail of 'IT operations technicians'. It is estimated that over the five years between 2003 and 2008 there will be a need for 6,000 new employees to fill vacancies in the broader occupational type of 'IT Service Delivery Occupations'. 2 out of every 20 employees work part time in this type of job.

Entry Routes and Training: There are no set routes into this career although most computer service technicians have Standard Grades or equivalent. Many have additional qualifications such as a National Certificate in computing.

SVQs are available at levels 1 to 3 in subjects including Operating IT Systems, Implementing Information Technology Solutions and Installing and Supporting IT Systems.

Qualifications: There are no minimum academic requirements for entry into this career. However, most entrants have Standard Grades, including Maths and English.

According to government statistics, employees in this type of job have the following qualifications. Higher Education: 5 out of 10 employees have their highest level of qualifications attained at degree level or equivalent or higher. Post-16 or Further Education: 2 out of 10 employees have their highest qualification at a level below a degree or higher degree or equivalent, but gained after the age of 16. School leaving age (16) qualifications or qualifications at SVQ3: 3 out of 10 employees gained their highest qualification at the age of 16 or have gained another qualification lower than a VQ level 3 since they were 16.

Computer Support Services Engineer

Computer support services engineers help customers with their computer needs. They install, demonstrate, maintain and update computer equipment. This work often involves travelling to the customer's home or business premises. Some support services engineers staff telephone helplines.

Work Activities: Computer support services engineers help customers to get the best performance from their computer equipment and overcome any technical problems they have in using it. They demonstrate, install and maintain hardware/ software systems, products and services and their 'upgrades' (improved versions).

Support services engineers give advice on all aspects of the installation and use of computers. They may provide support through a telephone help line, answering the whole range of customers' enquiries from simple questions to complex, highly technical problems.

Some support engineers install software on customers' premises, making sure that it works. Under aftersales service contracts, they provide regular maintenance and servicing of the computer equipment to minimise breakdowns and malfunctions.

This work involves routine testing, identification of faults and, where this is relatively straightforward, the replacement of faulty components. If the computer breaks down during operation, a computer support services engineer visits the customers' premises to diagnose and repair any minor faults on-site. They may have to refer more complex faults back to the manufacturer. Through working with customers, support engineers identify potential software development and sales opportunities for the future.

Computer support services engineers may also produce technical material including manuals to help customers understand their software.

They may be required to travel to clients' premises locally or nationally.

Personal Qualities and Skills: You need a sound technical background in practical electronics. You need to be knowledgeable about the products or services provided to customers. You must keep up-to-date with new developments. You'll need to understand both hardware and software; both can cause operating faults.

You'll need strong communication skills, tact and consideration to work with both technical and non-technical clients. You need to keep clear and up-to-date records and report faults back to your customer service manager or service engineer manager for any further action.

Pay and Opportunities: Salaries for engineers vary. The pay rates given below are approximate. Salaries for computer support services engineers are in the range of £14,500—£17,500 a year, rising to £22,500—£27,500. Higher earners can make around £35,500 a year. Salaries may include performance-related pay, profit sharing or company bonuses.

Computer support services engineers typically work 35 hours Monday to Friday, but early starts, late finishes, on-call and weekend work may be required.

Employers, throughout the UK, vary from large multinational corporations to small computer-system suppliers.

The following information is sourced from government statistics. The government's definition of types of job is slightly different to that used in this programme. For this type of job, the most relevant government-defined occupation is 'Computer engineers, installation and maintenance'.

In 2001 there were 2,200 people working as 'Computer engineers, installation and maintenance' in Scotland. 10 in every 10,000 employees working in Scotland were employed as 'Computer engineers, installation and maintenance'.

Estimates of projected future job openings requiring new entrants to the jobs market are available, but not at the level of detail of 'Computer engineers, installation and maintenance'. Employment levels for the broader occupational type of 'Electrical Trades' are projected to decline over the five years between 2003 and 2008 and there will be limited job opportunities for new employees.

1 out of every 20 employees works part time in this type of job.

Entry Routes and Training: A relevant degree or Higher National Diploma is often an advantage, although there is no formal academic requirement for entry to this work. In general, technical degrees such as Electronic Engineering and Computer Science are preferred for management positions. Most training is given on the job.

Modern Apprenticeships, leading to SVQ level 3, may be available in your area.

Qualifications: There is no formal academic requirement for entry into this career. However, most entrants have at least Standard Grades (1-3) including Maths and English. Many have additional qualifications including a Higher National Certificate/Higher National Diploma or a degree in, for example, Electronic Engineering.

According to government statistics, employees in this type of job have the following qualifications. Higher Education: 1 out of 10 employees have their highest level of qualifications attained at degree level or equivalent or higher. Post-16 or Further Education: 6 out of 10 employees have their highest qualification at a level below a degree or higher degree or equivalent, but gained after the age of 16. School leaving age (16) qualifications or qualifications at SVQ3: 3 out of 10 employees gained their highest qualification at the age of 16 or have gained another qualification lower than a VQ level 3 since they were 16.

Computer Technical Sales Manager

Computer technical sales managers sell computer hardware and software to commercial customers. They give advice about appropriate equipment. The work may involve negotiating contracts. They also provide an after-sales service.

Work Activities: Computer technical sales managers are responsible for the sale of computer hardware and software to other organisations. They persuade customers that they will benefit from buying new computer systems or adding to the systems that they already have. To do this, technical sales managers have to understand the customer's organisation. They work out what the customer needs to help their business run smoothly and then choose a computer system to help them achieve this.

Technical sales managers need to give a lot of information to the customer. For example, they tell them what effect new systems will have on their organisation. They also prepare reports and presentations to persuade managers to buy their products.

When they have made a sale, technical sales managers keep in contact with the customer after the installation of the system, providing technical advice and support in case problems develop. This contact also enables them to find out if the organisation has any further need for new computer equipment.

You may need to travel locally or nationally.

Personal Qualities and Skills: As a computer technical sales manager, you will need excellent communication skills. You must be able to describe or explain technical ideas in everyday language. The ability to persuade and negotiate is very important, as are patience and persistence because some negotiations last several months.

Pay and Opportunities: Salaries for computer technical sales managers vary widely depending on the size and type of company they work for. The pay rates given below are approximate. Sales managers earn in the range of £24,000—£30,000 a year, rising to £40,000—£57,000. Higher earners can make around £80,000 a year. Salaries may include performance-related pay, profit sharing or company bonuses.

Technical sales managers usually work office hours, Monday to Friday. However, you may need to do early starts and late finishes from time to time and occasional nights away from home.

Employers, throughout the UK, are manufacturers of computers and/or related equipment, dealers, software houses or consultancies. They may specialise in a particular market, such as health care.

The following information is sourced from government statistics. The government's definition of types of job is slightly different to that used in this programme. For this type of job, the most relevant Government-defined occupation is 'Marketing and sales managers'.

In 2001 there were 20,900 people working as 'Marketing and sales managers' in Scotland. 97 in every 10,000 employees working in Scotland were employed as 'Marketing and sales managers'.

Estimates of projected future job openings requiring new entrants to the jobs market are available, but not at the level of detail of 'Marketing and sales managers'. It is estimated that over the five years between 2003 and 2008 there will be a need for 21,000 new employees to fill vacancies in the broader occupational type of 'Functional Managers'.

1 out of every 20 employees works part time in this type of job.

Entry Routes and Training: Direct entrants to technical sales are likely to need a degree or Higher National Diploma (computer science or other technical subjects may be preferred), but Highers may be enough for less technically complex products.

People often enter sales work as a career change or development from other work in the computer industry, such as systems analysis. People with degrees and HNDs in business and marketing related qualifications also enter this career.

If you are completely new to computing work, you will follow an extensive training programme. Such programmes cover product and company knowledge, understanding the business world in general terms, learning about existing and potential customers and selling and negotiating skills. You may receive training in-house; regular training throughout your career is essential to keep you up to date with technical developments.

Qualifications: For entry to a degree course the minimum requirement is 3 Highers (A-C) plus Standard Grades (1-3) in 2 other subjects.

However, entry requirements vary between courses and alternative qualifications may be accepted—check prospectuses for details.

Higher National Diplomas/Higher National Certificates and degrees in non-computing subjects could be relevant for employment.

According to government statistics, people working in this type of job have the following qualifications. Higher Education: 6 out of 10 employees have their highest level of qualifications attained at degree level or equivalent or higher. Post-16 or Further Education: 2 out of 10 employees have their highest qualification at a level below a degree or higher degree or equivalent, but gained after the age of 16. School leaving age (16) qualifications or qualifications at SVQ3: 3 out of 10 employees gained their highest qualification at the age of 16 or have gained another qualification lower than a VQ level 3 since they were 16.

Computer/IT Support Manager

Computer/IT support managers are responsible for the provision of IT (Information Technology) advice and support to IT users within their organisation.

Work Activities: Computer/IT support managers are responsible for the provision of IT advice and support to IT users within their organisation. Typically, they manage a small team of staff, who may include helpline operators, computer service technicians and network technicians/administrators.

They work for a wide range of organisations, ranging from private sector companies to local government and the civil service.

Particularly in smaller departments, computer/IT support managers may provide some day-to-day support themselves. This may involve them working on a 'helpdesk', taking calls from users, getting details of problems they may be experiencing and talking them through the steps necessary to resolve them. In many cases, telephone advice may be enough, but in others, they may have to go to the user's own office and work directly on their computer.

An important aspect of their work is managing the staff and the resources of their section or department. These responsibilities are likely to include such matters as:

- Recruiting new staff.
- Organising helpdesk rotas.
- Budgeting and forward planning.
- Organising and (in some cases) delivering training.
- Preparing management reports, *e.g.* on the number and nature of support requests received.
- Reviewing the effectiveness of existing systems.

They may also be involved in deciding which hardware/software to buy to meet the organisation's needs. Other responsibilities can include negotiating service level agreements with external suppliers of IT-related services and disaster recovery if the system crashes (breaks down).

When problems arise due to technical issues, computer/IT support managers work with other IT staff within the organisation to resolve them. These include the computer network manager/administrator when a network-related problem arises. They may also have to liaise with external hardware and software suppliers and specialist agencies such as internet access providers.

When the introduction of new hardware or software is planned, computer/IT support managers need to become familiar with this as soon as possible (or delegate a member of the staff team to become familiar with it), so that they can provide the right level of support to users. They may be asked to advise on the introduction of new systems and often become members of planning/consultative groups concerning the use of new technology. They need to keep up to date with developments in the IT field, as changes are happening all the time.

Finally, some computer/IT support managers also take responsibility for network management. This means that, as well as the duties listed above, they are also responsible for the efficient and secure operation of any computer networks used within their organisation.

Personal Qualities and Skills: As a computer/IT support manager, you will need an interest in computers and a detailed knowledge of computer hardware and software. You will also need good business knowledge and management skills.

You will require a patient, methodical approach, as identifying the cause of a user's problem sometimes requires a degree of detective work.

For managing staff and liaising with users and suppliers, good written and spoken communication skills are important.

You will need to be calm and conscientious and able to cope with a degree of stress, especially when problems arise (such as network failures) that are outside your control.

Pay and Opportunities: The pay rates given below are approximate. Salaries for support managers are in the range of £24,500—£32,000 a year, rising to £42,500—£57,000. Higher earners can make around £76,000 a year. Salaries may include performance related pay, profit sharing or company bonuses.

Computer/IT support managers usually work a basic 37-hour week, Monday to Friday. Late finishes and weekend work may be required and in some circumstances, they may be called out to deal with emergencies.

Jobs exist throughout the UK with employers in industry and commerce, including banks, building societies and insurance companies and in the public sector with local and central government departments, the NHS and public utilities. Some experienced support managers work on a freelance basis—usually on short term contracts.

The following information is sourced from government statistics. The government's definition of types of job is slightly different to that used in this programme. For this type of job, the most relevant Government-defined occupation is 'Information and communication technology managers'.

In 2001 there were 9,400 people working as 'Information and communication technology managers' in Scotland. 43 in every 10,000 employees working in Scotland were employed as 'Information and communication technology managers'.

Estimates of projected future job openings requiring new entrants to the jobs market are available, but not at the level of detail of 'Information and communication technology managers'. It is estimated that over the five years between 2003 and 2008 there will be a need for 21,000 new employees to fill vacancies in the broader occupational type of 'Functional Managers'.

1 out of every 20 employees works part time in this type of job.

Entry Routes and Training: Most computer /IT support managers possess a relevant degree or Higher National Diploma.

Those planning a career in IT are advised to take a degree or HND course accredited by the British Computer Society. Different courses have different emphases and it is important to check the prospectuses of the institutions concerned to identify those courses most likely to meet your future career aspirations. For computer/IT support management, relevant topics would include computer systems architecture, systems analysis and design and human-computer interaction. This is not normally an entry-level job, however and you would usually gain experience in a role such as systems analyst or network administrator before obtaining a position as a computer/IT support manager.

Many computer/IT support managers study part-time for further qualifications, for example the professional qualifications of the British Computer Society (BCS) and the Institute for the

Management of Information Systems (IMIS). These can be studied full time or part time, by distance learning or at a local college.

They may also study for qualifications relevant to the specific networks and systems used in their organisation, *e.g.* Microsoft Certified Support Engineer (MCSE) or Certified Novell Engineer (CNE). Studying for these qualifications typically involves attending short, intensive courses at specially accredited training centres.

They are also likely to have to attend short courses provided by suppliers and external training organisations to help familiarise them with new hardware and software prior to its introduction within their organisation.

Qualifications: Most computer/IT support managers are graduates. Employers are also likely to want you to have experience in a role such as systems analyst or network administrator.

For entry to a degree course the minimum requirement is 3 Highers (A-C) plus Standard Grades in 2 other subjects.

However, entry requirements vary between course and alternative qualifications may be accepted—check prospectuses for details.

According to government statistics, people working in this type of job have the following qualifications. Higher Education: 6 out of 10 employees have their highest level of qualifications attained at degree level or equivalent or higher. Post-16 or Further Education: 2 out of 10 employees have their highest qualification at a level below a degree or higher degree or equivalent, but gained after the age of 16. School leaving age (16) qualifications or qualifications at SVQ3: 3 out of 10 employees gained their highest qualification at the age of 16 or have gained another qualification lower than a VQ level 3 since they were 16.

Computer/Software Sales Assistant

Computer/software sales assistants work in stores selling computers and computer-related goods. They help customers choose the products that best meet their needs and perform all the tasks necessary to complete the sale.

Work Activities: Computer/software sales assistants work in stores selling computers and computer-related goods. They help customers choose those products which would best meet their needs and perform all the tasks necessary to complete the sale. The range of products likely to be on offer in a computer/ software store include:

- computers
- printers
- scanners
- accessories
- consumables (paper, toner cartridges, etc.)
- books on computing
- computer software (such as word processing packages and games).

Many customers will not have a detailed knowledge of computers, so the assistant may need to spend a while talking to them to find out their needs. Customers may be planning to spend hundreds or even thousands of pounds so they will expect in-depth information and informed advice. In many cases, the customer will also want the assistant to demonstrate the hardware or software concerned.

When a sale has been made, assistants take the payment and record the sale on an electronic cash register. Where a customer pays by cheque or debit/credit card, the assistant will need to get payment authorisation from the card company or via a cheque clearance agency such as Transax. At the end of the transaction, the assistant will give the customer a detailed receipt and perhaps a separate guarantee.

As well as their direct selling responsibilities, computer/ software shop assistants are generally expected to perform a range of other duties. These may include:

- dusting and tidying the products on display
- replacing products sold with new products from the stockroom

- setting up display machines and making sure they work properly
- unpacking deliveries from suppliers or the company warehouse
- checking that all goods on display have price tickets and security tags
- dealing with customer complaints and returned goods
- keeping an eye open for shoplifters.

Many computer/software shops also have associated mail order and Internet operations. In such cases, assistants' responsibilities may also include taking telephone orders and enquiries, answering letters and emails, processing orders and general post room duties.

Personal Qualities and Skills: As a computer/software sales assistant, you will need an interest in computers and a good knowledge of the products on sale (training will be provided in this). You will need to be clean and tidy in appearance and friendly and polite.

Good communication skills are essential, both when listening to customers to try to understand their needs and when explaining sometimes complex technical matters to them. You will need to remain calm and courteous at all times, even when you are under pressure or feel that a complaining customer is in the wrong.

You must enjoy working in a close-knit team and be prepared to be adaptable, covering other people's jobs when they are off sick or on holiday and willing to move at short notice to another section or department if you are needed. Like all shop workers, you will need to be punctual and trustworthy.

Finally, physical fitness/stamina is important, as computer/ software shop assistants are on their feet for most of the day. They may also be required to carry heavy boxes containing computers and other equipment to and from the stockroom and to customers' cars.

Pay and Opportunities: Computer/software sales assistants earn in the range of £180—£200 a week, rising to £250—£310. Higher earners can make around £430 a week.

Sales assistants usually work a basic 35—39 hours per week. However, they may be required to work in the evenings or at weekends and receive overtime pay or time off in lieu. Many retail assistants are employed on a part-time basis and there may be opportunities for casual work during busy periods, for example, at Christmas.

Computer sales assistants work in a range of outlets: small specialist computer shops, chain stores selling electronic goods, office supply companies and even supermarkets and large department stores.

Promotion opportunities, depending on experience, are available with most of the larger employers.

The following information is sourced from government statistics. The government's definition of types of job is slightly different to that used in this programme. For this type of job, the most relevant Government-defined occupation is 'Sales and retail assistants'.

In 2001 there were 95,900 people working as 'Sales and retail assistants' in Scotland. 44 in every 1,000 employees working in Scotland were employed as 'Sales and retail assistants'.

Entry Routes and Training: There are no formal entry requirements for this occupation.

Computer/software sales assistants are trained by their employers in matters such as product knowledge, customer service and use of the cash register. In large stores, a group of trainees starting at the same time may complete an induction course conducted by the training manager away from the sales floor. Assistants may also attend short product knowledge courses run by major suppliers such as computer manufacturers.

New entrants may be able to train through a Skillseekers/ Modern Apprenticeship. This combines on-the-job training with off-the-job training at a college or training centre and leads to SVQ levels 2/3.

Qualifications: Requirements vary for entry to this work depending on the company you apply to work for. It may be possible to enter this occupation without any formal educational qualifications, but often employers prefer applicants to have some Standard Grades (1-3) including Maths and English.

Data Input Operator

Data input operators use a keyboard to type data into computers. They deal with text and numerical data, putting the information in the required format. Many operators also have other office duties.

Work Activities: Data input operators transfer written information into a computer or visual display unit (VDU), so that it can be stored in the machine's memory. Eventually, someone can retrieve the information on screen or print it out on paper. Data input operators may deal with words, for example, reports, lists and standard letters, or with numerical data on spreadsheets.

The operator types or 'keys in' these details according to a set format. Often, they input data into spaces or 'fields' on the computer. A simple example is an address list, where the operator enters a person's first name into one field, the surname into another, the postcode into another and so on.

Sometimes operators input the data in code form. For example, they may key in standard information such as a commonly used street name under a one or two digit code. By inputting the information in exactly the right order, operators enable others to recall data for specific tasks, for example, printing off quarterly sales figures.

Many data input operators also spend part of their time on other office duties like word processing and clerical tasks.

Personal Qualities and Skills: As a data input operator, you should be able to work quickly and accurately, often under pressure or to a deadline. The work can sometimes be monotonous but still needs good powers of concentration and attention to detail.

This work may present difficulties for anyone who suffers from eye strain or poor eyesight, because it involves constant use of a computer screen. You will also be dealing with a variety of paperwork.

You'll need to have good literacy and number skills. Ideally, you should also have a fairly logical mind and some understanding of how computers work. This will enable you to use a variety of different databases and to cope with any day-to-day problems with the system you are using.

You need keyboard or typing skills (at least 25—30 words per minute).

Pay and Opportunities: The pay rates given below are approximate. Starting salaries can depend on age and experience. Salaries are in the range of £11,000—£12,500 a year, rising to £15,000—£21,500. Higher earners can make around £24,000 a year.

Data input operators usually work 35—39 hours from Monday to Friday and some work shifts. Full-time, part-time, temporary and flexible working arrangements may be available.

Employment throughout the UK is with commercial organisations, some public utilities and government departments.

The following information is sourced from government statistics. The government's definition of types of job is slightly different to that used in this programme. For this type of job, the most relevant Government-defined occupation is 'Database assistants/clerks'.

In 2001 there were 4,100 people working as 'Database assistants/clerks' in Scotland. 19 in every 10,000 employees working in Scotland were employed as 'Database assistants/ clerks'.

Estimates of projected future job openings requiring new entrants to the jobs market are available, but not at the level of detail of 'Database assistants/clerks'. It is estimated that over the five years between 2003 and 2008 there will be a need for 7,000 new employees to fill vacancies in the broader occupational type of 'Administrative Occupations: Records'. 6 out of every 20 employees work part time in this type of job.

Entry Routes and Training: Entry routes vary depending on the type of data inputting involved. You may be able to enter this work directly but some employers prefer those who have taken a relevant college course.

Many entrants train through a Skillseekers/Modern Apprenticeship. This combines on-the-job training with off-the-job training at a college or training centre and leads to SVQ levels 2/3.

Qualifications: Employers may ask for 3/4 Standard Grades (1-3) including English. However, in some cases it may be possible to enter with no formal qualifications. Typing or keyboard skills of at least 25-30 words per minute are also required.

According to government statistics, employees in this type of job have the following qualifications. Higher Education: 2 out of 10 employees have their highest level of qualifications attained at degree level or equivalent or higher. Post-16 or Further Education: 2 out of 10 employees have their highest qualification at a level below a degree or higher degree or equivalent, but gained after the age of 16. School leaving age (16) qualifications or qualifications at SVQ3: 6 out of 10 employees gained their highest qualification at the age of 16 or have gained another qualification lower than a VQ level 3 since they were 16.

Multimedia Specialist

Multimedia specialists make computer programmes that use text, sound, graphics and pictures to entertain, educate or inform the user.

Work Activities: Multimedia specialists create products that use more than one way to communicate information. For example, they may use sound, text, graphics, animation and video pictures. They bring these different types of communication together using a computer. Multimedia specialists work on games, educational software, websites, film, television and video. Their products may go on CD-ROMS or the Internet.

Producing a multimedia product is a team effort. Writers, artists, graphic designers, animators and sound engineers make the content of the files. The multimedia specialist plays a vital role in translating this information into a language that the computer can understand.

Everyone works very closely together under the direction of a producer. As the work progresses, they attend meetings to discuss and sort out problems. Once the team has written the programme, multimedia specialists test it to identify and fix any errors they have found in the content or programme.

Multimedia specialists may design and write web pages, programme the links to company databases, or create graphic effects for film studios. Some multimedia specialists produce images for company presentations.

Personal Qualities and Skills: To be a multimedia specialist, you will need a strong interest in information technology, although it's just as important to be creative and enthusiastic. You will need an open mind to grasp the future possibilities of multimedia.

It is very important that you are a good team worker because multimedia specialists usually work in small project teams with other experts, including artists, graphic designers and sound engineers.

You'll need strong communication skills to swap ideas and to explain your work clearly and concisely to people who may not have much computer knowledge. You should enjoy solving problems and working on a project from start to finish.

Good organisational skills will help you to plan your work and to meet deadlines. You must be able to work well under pressure.

Pay and Opportunities: Starting salaries can depend on age and qualifications. The pay rates given below are approximate. Multimedia specialists earn in the range of £15,000—£17,500 a year, rising to £22,500—£27,500. Higher earners can make around £37,000 a year.

Multimedia specialists usually work 35—37 hours Monday to Friday, although you may need to do some late finishes as deadlines approach.

There are opportunities with multimedia publishers, software producers, website design companies and television and film companies. Consultancy and fixed-term contract work can be available for experienced multimedia designers and programmers.

The following information is sourced from government statistics. The government's definition of types of job is slightly different to that used in this programme. For this type of job, the most relevant Government-defined occupation is 'Graphic designers'.

In 2001 there were 4,600 people working as 'Graphic designers' in Scotland. 21 in every 10,000 employees working in Scotland were employed as 'Graphic designers'.

Estimates of projected future job openings requiring new entrants to the jobs market are available, but not at the level of detail of 'Graphic designers'. It is estimated that over the five years between 2003 and 2008 there will be a need for 3,000 new employees to fill vacancies in the broader occupational type of 'Design Associate Professionals'.

3 out of every 20 employees work part time in this type of job.

Entry Routes and Training: Most people need a degree or Higher National Diploma in a relevant information technology subject to enter this career. Course titles vary, some having more emphasis on hardware issues, some on systems engineering and others on analysis and design. You must check college and university prospectuses carefully. Degree course titles include Multimedia Computing and Multimedia Design; there are HNDs with titles like Multimedia or Design Technology.

If you have a degree in a non-related subject, you could still find a way into this career. Some employers offer the chance to gain IT skills under graduate training programmes.

Qualifications: For entry to a degree course, the usual minimum requirement is 3 Highers (A-C) and Standard Grades (1-3) in 2 other subjects, including English.

However, entry requirements vary between courses and alternative qualifications may be accepted—check prospectuses for details.

According to government statistics, employees in this type of job have the following qualifications. Higher Education: 6 out of 10 employees have their highest level of qualifications attained at degree level or equivalent or higher. Post-16 or Further Education: 2 out of 10 employees have their highest qualification at a level below a degree or higher degree or equivalent, but gained after the age of 16. School leaving age (16) qualifications or qualifications at SVQ3: 2 out of 10 employees gained their highest qualification at the age of 16 or have gained another qualification lower than a VQ level 3 since they were 16.

Telecommunications Engineer

Telecommunications engineers work on the different types of technology that enable us to communicate over distance. They may deal with satellite and cable systems, mobile phones, radio waves, the Internet and electronic mail. The world of telecommunications is changing very rapidly; it involves very sophisticated equipment and the latest technology.

Work Activities: Telecommunications engineers research and develop innovative products, as well as working on ways to improve existing technology, like fibre optic cables. Some telecommunications companies design, build and install telecommunications systems for their clients.

Increasingly, networks are inter-linked; for example, engineers have developed systems where a mobile telephone user can access the Internet. Digital television systems can be interactive; users can have high-speed access to the Internet and e-mail.

Engineers may work on ways to provide solutions for business and private customers. For example, engineers may help a company to handle high volumes of telephone calls, perhaps by setting up or helping to improve a call centre. Engineers work closely with their clients, discussing solutions like Computer Telephony Integration (CTI).

Telecommunications engineers have installed video conferencing links in hospitals. Surgeons can perform operations under the supervision of experts at another hospital, using the video-link to hear and see their colleagues.

Engineers work on services like mobile communication, high-speed data and fax transmission and radio paging. They may install the equipment needed for these types of communication. Some engineers are responsible for routine maintenance and repair work, to make sure the system does not break down. Engineers may run centres or work on help desks, to respond quickly to repair or deal with any disruptions to the network.

Some telecommunications engineers travel around locally to make sure that all the sites of the network are working properly. They may use computer software to see if any part of the network is 'weak' and therefore more likely to break down.

Personal Qualities and Skills: You must be willing to learn and develop new knowledge, to keep up to date with advances in areas such as satellite technology, electronic commerce and mobile telephone networks.

Also, you must have an investigative mind and excellent problem solving skills. Telecommunications engineers need management and organisation skills, to plan networks. For example, they may need to map cable networks.

Some telecommunications engineers work closely with sales and marketing departments. They may answer customer enquiries and could be involved in selling networks to new clients. You therefore need the ability to build up comprehensive product knowledge; persuasive sales skills are useful.

Engineers need computer software skills because computers are often used to control telecommunications systems.

Pay and Opportunities: Salaries vary depending on the company and level of responsibility. The pay rates given below are approximate. Telecommunications engineers earn in the range of £21,500—£25,000 a year, rising to £31,000—£37,500. Higher earners can make around £46,500 a year.

Most work 35—40 hours, Monday to Friday. However, early starts, late finishes and some weekend work may be required.

Telecommunications engineers work in research and development, as well as manufacturing and installation.

Employers are public service providers who run the public telephone system, cable TV companies, cellular radio system providers and manufacturers of electronic communications products.

Companies with complex telecommunication requirements may employ their own engineers (for example, multinational oil companies).

Opportunities for telecommunications engineers are fast increasing as the industry expands into global markets.

The following information is sourced from government statistics. The government's definition of types of job is slightly different to that used in this programme. For this type of job, the most relevant government-defined occupation is 'Electrical engineers'.

In 2001 there were 1,500 people working as Electrical engineers in Scotland. 7 in every 10,000 employees working in Scotland were employed as Electrical engineers.

Entry Routes and Training: Telecommunications engineers usually complete an appropriate engineering degree or Higher National Diploma. There are a number of specialist courses, with titles like BSc Telecommunications Engineering at Glasgow Caledonian University and B.Eng Electronics and Electrical Engineering (Communications) available at Edinburgh University. UHI Millennium Institute offer a course in HND Engineering Telecommunications.

Many telecommunications engineers have backgrounds in electronic engineering, although entrants may also be graduates in other engineering disciplines, including mechanical engineering. Some entrants may also have backgrounds in computer science, mathematics and physics.

It is essential to consult prospectuses to make sure the course you choose is appropriate to the branch of engineering you want to follow. Many graduates go on to join manufacturers' Graduate Training Schemes, which offer structured training and learning.

Depending on their level of entry, telecommunications engineers can gain Chartered Engineer or Incorporated

Engineer status. Both are highly regarded by employers throughout industry.

Chartered Engineers (CEng) normally have the greatest level of responsibility for engineering projects. They plan and manage engineering activities and functions and lead the development of new technologies. They make sure that a project is completed on time and within budget. Chartered engineers work at the highest management levels.

Incorporated Engineers (IEng) normally have a specific level of responsibility for engineering projects. They may work as team leaders or deal with technical aspects of complex technologies. They may supervise quality assurance procedures and manage and develop test and inspection programmes. Incorporated engineers generally work at middle management levels and some of their work overlaps with that of Chartered Engineers.

To register with the Engineering Council (UK) as a Chartered Engineer (CEng) or Incorporated Engineer (IEng), you must apply through an appropriate engineering body.

The usual route to CEng status is to complete first an accredited degree in engineering, as listed on the Engineering Council (UK) website, *e.g.* an MEng.

The usual route to IEng status is to complete first an accredited degree in engineering, as listed on the Engineering Council (UK) website, *e.g.* a B.Eng.

After gaining your degree, you will undergo Initial Professional Development (IPD). This involves accredited training and responsible experience in the workplace, followed by a Professional Review with interview to assess your competence and your commitment to Continued Professional Development (CPD).

Qualifications: The usual qualification for entry into this career is a degree. However, it may be possible to enter with a Higher National Diploma or Higher National Certificate.

Entry to a relevant engineering degree is normally with 3/4 Highers (A-C) plus Standard Grades (1-3) in 1/2 other subjects. At Higher, Maths and a science subject (normally

Physics) are often preferred and may be essential. Entry to a relevant HNC/HND is normally with 1/3 Highers and Standard Grades.

Entry requirements vary between courses and alternative qualifications may be accepted—check prospectuses for details.

Website Designer

Website designers use a combination of design and IT skills to produce Web pages for the Internet. They need to achieve a balance between interesting design and ease of use.

Work Activities: Website designers use a combination of design and computer skills to produce websites for the Internet.

To create a website, designers have to think carefully about the end product (the user interface). They need to achieve a balance between attractive design and delivering clear, easy to understand information. The most successful sites allow people to travel around them easily. Many designers make their websites as interactive as possible. This means that there is a two-way flow of information between the user and the website; the computer responds to the user's requests.

Website designers can use a number of different ways to communicate information; this means that they use multimedia. For example, their website may have text, speech, graphics, animation or video pictures.

Website designers may use HTML (Hypertext Markup Language) to create text; they may use other programming languages, such as Java, to add a level of interactivity to a website. Also, they may use specialist Web design tools.

Some companies ask website designers to manage the sites they have created. They must make sure that site information is up-to-date and relevant. To do this, they work closely with colleagues, including public relations staff and software engineers.

Personal Qualities and Skills: To be a website designer, you must have a strong interest in information technology. It is equally important to have strong design skills and be creative and enthusiastic. You should be skilled in computer languages like HTML and Java, or be willing to learn and develop these skills.

You'll need an open mind to grasp the future potential of the Internet and to think about the best way to use multimedia technologies like graphics, video and sound.

Good teamwork skills are very important; you may be working closely with public relations staff, marketing departments or other IT specialists.

Designers who work on a freelance basis need the skills to run their own business.

Pay and Opportunities: The pay rates given below are approximate. Website designers earn in the range of £15,000—£17,500 a year, rising to £22,500—£27,500. Higher earners can make around £37,000 a year.

Website designers usually work 35—37 hours Monday to Friday, though some late finishes may be required as deadlines approach.

Opportunities occur with employers in every area of industry and commerce, including retail and broadcasting industries and charity organisations and in the public sector, in local and central government. Other opportunities are with advertising agencies and specialist website design agencies. Some designers work independently on a freelance basis.

Opportunities are increasing as more and more organisations realise the marketing potential of the Internet. Consultancy and fixed-term contract work can be available for experienced web designers, including through specialist IT recruitment agencies.

The following information is sourced from government statistics. The government's definition of types of job is slightly different to that used in this programme. For this type of job, the most relevant Government-defined occupation is 'Graphic designers'.

In 2001 there were 4,600 people working as 'Graphic designers' in Scotland. 21 in every 10,000 employees working in Scotland were employed as 'Graphic designers'.

Estimates of projected future job openings requiring new entrants to the jobs market are available, but not at the level of detail of 'Graphic designers'. It is estimated that over the five years between 2003 and 2008 there will be a need for 3,000 new employees to fill vacancies in the broader occupational type of 'Design Associate Professionals'.

3 out of every 20 employees work part time in this type of job.

Entry Routes and Training: There is no set route into this job. However, most entrants have a degree or Higher National Diploma in a computer related subject.

There is a variety of degree level courses that teach the combined skills of design and computing. They have titles like Multimedia Computing, Design with Multimedia Studies, Multimedia Graphics, Interactive Systems Design and Electronic Media Design.

HNDs that may be useful have course titles such as Multimedia Information Technology, Multimedia with Web Development and Electronic Graphics.

You may be able to enter this career with a degree in a non-IT subject; some employers give IT training to people with a background in more traditional design subjects.

Qualifications: This is a relatively new job, so there is no formally recognised pathway into it. Some people enter with a degree or Higher National Diploma in a computer or design related subject.

For entry to a degree course the minimum requirement is 3 Highers (A-C) plus Standard Grades (1-3) in 2 other subjects.

However, entry requirements vary between courses and alternative qualifications may be accepted—check prospectuses for details.

Prospective entrants to Design courses usually need to present a portfolio of examples of their work.

According to government statistics, employees in this type of job have the following qualifications. Higher Education: 6 out of 10 employees have their highest level of qualifications attained at degree level or equivalent or higher. Post-16 or Further Education: 2 out of 10 employees have their highest qualification at a level below a degree or higher degree or equivalent, but gained after the age of 16. School leaving age (16) qualifications or qualifications at SVQ3: 2 out of 10 employees gained their highest qualification at the age of 16 or have gained another qualification lower than a VQ level 3 since they were 16.

Website Manager

Website managers, also known as webmasters, are responsible for managing Internet Websites. They may also set up or design sites.

Work Activities: Website managers, also known as webmasters, manage Internet or Intranet websites. They may supervise other staff, work in a team, or work alone. The role of a website manager depends on the type and size of the organisation they work for.

Website managers may be involved in the design of a site, perhaps working closely with website designers, or they may take on the role of designer themselves. The manager makes sure that any additions to the site follow the existing style, for example, in terms of design, layout and structure.

They may also have to check that any new information on the site matches the existing editorial style. It's very important that information on the Internet is accurate and up-to-date.

Managers who design sites may use a number of different ways to communicate information; this means that they use multimedia. For example, their website may have text, speech, graphics, animation or video pictures. However, the manager must get the balance right. If the user spends too much time waiting for the site to download, they may not want to visit the site again.

Managers need to achieve a balance between attractive design and delivering clear, easy to understand information. The most successful sites allow people to travel around them easily. Managers may try to make their websites as interactive as possible. This means that there is a two-way flow of information between the user and the website; the computer responds to the user's requests.

The manager plans and organises the development of the website. They work with information technology staff, making sure they have the right web software tools to do their job. Managers also find out people's training and development needs, perhaps arranging for an external trainer to visit the company.

Website managers are responsible for the security of the website. In a commercial company, this means making sure that only authorised people can access customer's details, for example, addresses or credit card information.

Managers may also work with communications, public relations and marketing departments. For example, they try to find out about the users of the website. They may put together monthly statistics that show how many people visited the website over that period. This information helps the company to market its services more effectively. Managers who work on Intranet sites (the use of Internet technologies and e-mail facilities on a closed network, *i.e.* within a single company) talk to people throughout the company to find out what they want or expect their website to provide.

Personal Qualities and Skills: As a website manager, you must have a strong interest in information technology. You'll also need to be creative, enthusiastic and eager to keep up-to-date with this fast developing area.

The ability to work well with other people is essential. You'll also need good communication skills to explain website development to people who may not have much knowledge of computers. Good written skills will help you to produce reports. You should also have good number skills to put together statistics, for example, to show how many people have used the site over a period of time.

If you are involved in website design, you should be skilled in computer languages like HTML (Hypertext MarkUp Language) and Java, or be willing to learn and develop these skills. You'll need an open mind to grasp the future potential of the Internet and think about the best way to use multimedia technologies like graphics, video and sound.

Website managers need a strong sense of responsibility. It will be up to you to arrange backup systems in case technology goes wrong; you must be able to stay calm under pressure. You'll need good organisation skills to plan your work and meet deadlines.

Website managers who work on a freelance basis need the skills to run their own business.

Pay and Opportunities: The pay rates given below are approximate. Website managers earn in the range of £17,000—£21,000 a year, rising to £27,500—£35,500. Higher earners can make around £45,000 a year. Salaries may include performance related pay, profit sharing or bonuses.

Website managers usually work 35—40 hours Monday to Friday, although you may do some late finishes to make sure information on the site is current.

Opportunities occur with employers in every area of industry and commerce, including retail and broadcasting industries and charity organisations and in the public sector, in local and central government.

Other opportunities are with advertising agencies and specialist website design agencies. Some website managers work independently on a freelance basis. Opportunities are increasing as more and more organisations realise the marketing potential of the Internet. Consultancy and fixed-term contract work can be available for experienced website designers, including through specialist IT recruitment agencies.

The following information is sourced from government statistics. The government's definition of types of job is slightly different to that used in this programme. For this type of job, the most relevant Government-defined occupation is 'IT operations technicians'.

In 2001 there were 7,500 people working as 'IT operations technicians' in Scotland. 35 in every 10,000 employees working in Scotland were employed as 'IT operations technicians'.

Estimates of projected future job openings requiring new entrants to the jobs market are available, but not at the level of detail of 'IT operations technicians'. It is estimated that over the five years between 2003 and 2008 there will be a need for 6,000 new employees to fill vacancies in the broader occupational type of 'IT Service Delivery Occupations'. 2 out of every 20 employees work part time in this type of job.

Entry Routes and Training: There is no set route into this career, although it is possible that experience in website design could lead into a website management role.

You'll usually need a background in computers, although some organisations may recruit people from marketing or public relations backgrounds.

Some employers will ask for computer related qualifications, while others will focus more on your past experience. There are lots of Higher National Diploma and degree courses that cover relevant areas.

Qualifications: As this is a relatively new job, there is no formally recognised pathway into it. However, there are a variety of degree courses that cover relevant topics, including Computer Science and Multimedia Computing courses.

For entry to a degree course the minimum requirement is 3 Highers (A-C) plus Standard Grades in 2 other subjects.

However, entry requirements vary between courses and alternative qualifications may be accepted—check prospectuses for details.

According to government statistics, employees in this type of job have the following qualifications. Higher Education: 5 out of 10 employees have their highest level of qualifications attained at degree level or equivalent or higher. Post-16 or Further Education: 2 out of 10 employees have their highest qualification at a level below a degree or higher degree or equivalent, but gained after the age of 16. School leaving age (16) qualifications or qualifications at SVQ3: 3 out of 10 employees gained their highest qualification at the age of 16 or have gained another qualification lower than a VQ level 3 since they were 16.

Information Technology Officer

This could be a mission statement for any local authority:

"To develop the technical infrastructure and environment

for all council services to flourish using information technology as a cornerstone to the business."

In local government, IT is central to the council's ability to deliver a quality service to the taxpayer.

IT officers work in small teams that provide desktop services to every department. The role may also include some IT related administration such as maintaining hardware and software inventories and internal invoicing. The post exists in all types of authority.

Work Environment: The work is office-based. In an average situation, technical officers will operate mixtures of mainframe, UNIX, Windows 95/98, Windows 2000, NT v 4 and Server 2000 platforms supporting corporate and business unit applications in a TCP/IP network environment utilizing LAN and WAN technology.

The standard working week is 37 hours and may allow flexitime and job share.

Daily Activities: IT services provide infrastructure and support to council members, officers and numerous software suppliers. The unit delivers access to corporate data through a communications network which also reaches officials' homes as well as offices (some remote) in the area.

On a daily basis, information technology officers help with evaluating IT solutions and advise service units on the use of technology within the following key areas of activity, as directed by the supervisor. Each requires different skills.

Strategy and consultancy service provides strategic guidance and direction on how information systems can be developed for the benefit of the whole council, but especially the business needs of its cost centre managers.

Project management service provides technical guidance and direction on possible IS systems and IT solutions for the business needs of the council. It is also involved with tendering procedures.

Systems development service incorporates developments, enhancements, corrective and legislative changes into existing applications. It also customises most packages supplied by third party vendors.

Technical support service ensures uninterrupted access to front line systems. It covers the provision, evaluation, management, maintenance and support of software, in particular operating systems and their security in a live environment.

Operations service provides operational support for full access to online systems and to help meet processing deadlines

Network service is available 24 hours per day, seven days a week. The service provides critical data quickly and securely and monitors traffic levels to ensure they do not jeopardise service availability. NS also covers Internet, Intranet, external and internal e-mail, virus and security control services.

Help desk support service covers the help and advice needed on the use of PCs and associated peripherals and software and their maintenance (including hardware). The aim is to ensure that the council has a high quality reactive support service, using technology to best effect.

IT officers are also responsible for keeping accurate records for service performance targets.

Skills & Interests: You would need to be:

- a team player
- committed to good service
- organised, carrying out work in a methodical and well documented way
- able to communicate effectively with all levels of staff both verbally and written.

Entry Requirements: 'A' Level in a computer discipline or equivalent and at least one year's experience working within a computing environment is are essential.

Estimated Salary Range: £10,278—£16,203

Please note that salary information is a guide only and there may be local agreements in place. For further information about salaries for particular positions, please contact your local council directly.

Future Prospects & Opportunities: There are always opportunities for advancement in information technology. In IT Services the next step up is Supervisor. With further training and experience, it is possible to aim for other posts such as Information Systems Officer and IT Helpdesk Coordinator.

There are opportunities in the private sector, too.

What should I do Next?: Look for current local government Information Technology Officer vacancies in the following places:

- LG jobs.com—the official recruitment website for local government.
- Weekly, bi-weekly or monthly jobs bulletins produced by local councils themselves, available from libraries, community centres, town halls/main civic buildings and central council personnel departments.
- Local council websites.
- Local newspapers
- National newspapers—The Guardian is particularly well known for its public sector job advertisements on a Wednesday.

Find out about the council and get some work experience if possible by:

- Making the most of work experience placements arranged through your school, college or university.
- Contacting councils close to your home to find out about the work experience opportunities they offer.
- Talking to someone who does the job you are interested in—ring your local council to see if someone can spare some time.
- Making an appointment to see a careers adviser for more specific information about jobs and training.

Bibliography

Albarran, Alan B. and Gregory G. Pitts: *The Radio Broadcasting Industry*, Boston, Allyn and Bacon, 2001.

Albrecht, Ulrich: *A Short Research Guide on Arms and Armed Forces*, New York, Facts on File, 1980.

Alexander, James: *Internships in Communications, Ames*, Iowa State University Press, 1995.

Allman, Paul: *Careers in Video and Digital Video*, New York: Rosen, 2001.

Anders, Peter: *Envisioning Cyberspace*, New York, McGraw-Hill, 1999.

Arkin, William M.: *Research Guide to Current Military and Strategic Affairs*, Washington, Institute for Policy Studies, 1981.

Baehr, H. and Gary A.: *Turning In On: A Reader in Women and Media*, London, Arnold, 1996.

Ball, Victoria Kloss: *Opportunities in Interior Design and Decorating Careers*, Chicago, VGM Career Horizons, 2002.

Barnouw, Erik: *A Tower in Babel: the History of Broadcasting in the United States to 1933*, New York, Oxford University Press, 1966.

Baucom, Alfred H.: *Hospitality Design for the Graying Generation: Meeting the Needs of a Growing Market*, New York, Wiley, 1996.

Baxter, John: *Australian Cinema*, Sydney, Pacific Books, 1970.

Beaman, Jim: *Interviewing for Radio*, New York, Routledge, 2000.

Berkowitz, Ira: *Vault Career Guide to Advertising*, New York, Vault, 2004.

Bertrand, Ina and Diane Collins: *Government and Film in Australia*, Sydney, Currency Press, 1981.

Bliss, Edward and James L. Hoyt: *Writing News for Broadcast*, New York, Columbia University Press, 1994.

Boella, Michael John: *Principles of Hospitality Law*, London, Cassell, 1999.

Bone, Jan, & Ana Fernandez: *Opportunities in Film Careers*, New York, VGM Career Books, 2004.

Bowers, C. A.: *The Cultural Dimension of Educational Computing: Understanding the Non-neutrality of Technology*, New York, Teachers' College Press; 1988.

Boyd, Andrew: *Broadcast Journalism: Techniques of Radio and TV News*, Woburn, Focal Press, 2001.

Brown, Douglas Robert: *The Restaurant Managers Handbook: How to Set Up, Operate, and Manage a Financially Successful Restaurant.* Lauderhill, Atlantic Pub., 1991.

Brown, James and Quaal Ward: *Radio-Television-Cable Management*, New York, McGraw Hill, 1998.

Bryant, Jennings: *Television and the American Family*, Hillsdale, Lawrence Erlbaum, 1990.

Buckingham, David: *Young People and the Media*, New York, Manchester University Press, 1993.

Buckner, Robert W.: *Site Selection: New Advancements in Methods and Technology*, New York, Lebhar-Friedman Books, 1998.

Caldwell, J. T.: *Electronic Media and Technoculture*, New Brusnwick, Rutgers University Press, 2000.

Careers in Focus: *Photography*, New York, Ferguson, 2004.

Carmouche, Rita: *Behavioural Studies in Hospitality Management*, New York, Chapman & Hall, 1995.

Carroll, Victoria: *Writing News for Television*, Ames, Iowa State University Press, 1997.

Cassiday, Doris, and Bruce Cassiday: *Careers in the Beauty Industry*, New York, Franklin Watts, 1978.

Clark, Mona: *Interpersonal Skills for Hospitality Managers*, London, Chapman Hill, 1995.

Clark, Roy Peter: *A Journalist Teaches Young Writers*, Portsmouth, Heinemann, 1987.

Cockburn, C. and Ormrod, S.: *Gender and Technology in the Making*, London, Sage, 1993.

Cohler, David Keith: *Broadcast Newswriting*, Englewood Cliffs, Prentice Hall, 1990.

Cracknell, H. L.: *Escoffier: The Complete Guide to the Art of Modern Cookery*, New York, John Wiley, 1979.

Craig, James: *Graphic Design Career Guide*, New York, Watson-Guptill, 1992.

Crawford, Tad: *Starting Your Career As a Freelance Photographer*, New York, Allworth Press, 2003.

Crouse, Chuck: *Reporting for Radio*, Chicago, Bonus Books, 1998.

Davidson, M. J. and Cooper, C. L.: *Women and Information Technology*, New York, John Wiley & Sons, 1987.

Delaney, Chuck: *Photography Your Way*, New York, Allworth Press, 2005.

Dennis, Everette E. and Edward C. Pease: *Children and the Media*, New Brunswick, Transaction Publishers, 1996.

Diamond, S. Taylor's Way: *Women, Cultures and Technology*, New York: Routledge; 1997.

Donald, Ralph and Thomas Spann: *Fundamentals of Television Production*, Ames, Iowa State University Press, 2000.

Dornenburg, Andrew: *Culinary Artistry*, New York, John Wiley & Sons, 1996.

Douglas, George H.: *The Early Days of Radio Broadcasting*, Jefferson, NC: McFarland, 1987.

Easlea, B.: *Fathering the Unthinkable: Masculinity, Scientists and the Nuclear Arms Race*, London, Pluto Press, 1982.

Ellis, Elmo: *Opportunities in Broadcasting Careers*, Chicago, VGM Career Books, 2005.

Faulkner, W. and Arnold, E.: *Smothered by Invention: Technology in Women's Lives*, London, Pluto Press, 1985.

Fensch, Thomas: *Television News Anchors*, Jefferson, McFarland, 1993.

Field, Shelly: *Career Opportunities in Advertising and Public Relations*, New York, Ferguson, 2006.

Foster, Timothy R. V.: *How to Succeed As an Independent Consultant*, London: Kogan, Page, 2002.

Fox Keller, E.: *Reflections on Gender and Science*, New Haven, Yale University Press, 1985.

Gardner, Garth: *Careers in Computer Graphics and Animation*, Fairfax, GGC, 2001.

Gibbs, Jenny: *Interior Design*, New York, H. N. Abrams, 2005.

Go, Frank M.: *Human Resource Management in the Hospitality Industry*, New York, Wiley, 1996.

Goldfarb, Roz: *Careers by Design*, New York, Allworth Press, 2001.

Gordon, Sandra R.: *Great Jobs for Film Majors*, Chicago, VGM Career Books, 2004.

Graham, Duane: *The Remarkable Story of Otto Graham*, Wayne, Immortal Investments Publishing, 2004.

Green, E. and Adam, A. Virtual Gender: *Technology, Consumption, and Identity*, New York, Routledge, 2001.

Greenman, Robert: *The Adviser's Companion*, New York, Columbia Scholastic Press Association, 1991.

Griffiths, D.: *The Exclusion of Women from Technology*, London, Pluto Press, 1985.

Hall, Ken G.: *Australian Film: the Inside Story*, Sydney, Summit Books, 1980.

Hewitt, John: *Airwords: Writing for Broadcast News, Mountain View*, Oxford, Mayfield Pub. Company, 2002.

Higham, Robin: *A Guide to the Sources of United States Military History*, Hamden, Archon Books, 1975.

Hilliard, Robert L. and Michael C. Keith: *The Broadcast Century and Beyond*, Boston: Focal Press, 2001.

Hinkin, Timothy R.: *Cases in Hospitality Management: A Critical Incident Approach*, New York, Wiley, 1995.

Holloway, J. C. : *Towards a Core Curriculum for Tourism: A Discussion Paper*, London, The National Liaison Group for Higher Education in Tourism, 1995.

Horstede, G.: *Cultures and Organizations: Software of the Mind*, London, McGraw-Hill Book Company, 1991.

Hungerland, Buff: *Marketing Your Creative Portfolio*, Upper Saddle River, Prentice Hall, 2003

Jain, S. C.: *Women and Technology*, Jaipur, Rawat Publications, 1985.

Jefferson, Michael: *Breaking into Graphic Design*, New York, Allworth Press, 2005.

Jensen, Clayne R.: *Opportunities in Recreation and Leisure Careers*, Lincolnwood, VGM Career Horizons, 2000.

Jones, Sue Jenklyn: *Fashion Design*, New York, Watson-Guptill, 2002.

Kieffer, John: *The Photographer's Assistant*, New York, Allworth, 2001.

Kirkham, P.: *The Gendered Object*, Manchester, Manchester University Press, 1996.

Kissane, Sharon F.: *Career Success for People with Physical Disabilities*, Lincolnwood, VGM Career Horizons, 1997.

Kring, Robin: *Party Creations: Book of Theme Event Design*, Denver, Clear Creek Pub., 1993.

Kurzweil, R.: *The Age of Spiritual Machines*, New York, Viking, 1999.

Lavery, P.: *Tourism Marketing and Management Handbook*, New York, Prentice Hall, 1989.

Lewis, Robert C.: *Cases in Hospitality Marketing and Management*, New York, John Wiley, 1997.

MacCloskey, Monro: *How to Qualify for the Service Academies*, New York, Richards Rosen Press, 1964.

Maclay, Edgar Stanton: *A History of the United States Navy 1771-1893*, New York, Appleton Co., 1894.

Mauro, Lucia: *Careers for Fashion Plates and Other Trendsetters*, Chicago, VGM Career Horizons, 2003.

McGuire-Lytle, Erin: *Careers in Graphic Arts and Computer Graphics*, New York, Rosen, 1999.

Miller, Samuel D.: *An Aerospace Bibliography*, Washington. Office of Air Force History, 1978.

Mitchell, Leslie Scott: *Freelancing for Television and Radio*, London; Routledge, 2005.

Mogel, Leonard: *Creating Your Career in Communications and Entertainment*, Sewickley, GATF Press, 1998.

Noronha, Shonan F. R.: *Opportunities in Television and Video Careers*, Chicago: VGM Career Books, 2003.

Orlik, Peter B.: *Career Perspectives in Electronic Media*, Ames, Blackwell Pub., 2004.

Packard, Sidney: *The Fashion Business: Dynamics and Careers*, New York, Holt, Rinehart, and Winston, 1983.

Parks, Peggy J.: *The News Media*, San Diego, Lucent Books, 2002.

Paullin, C.O.: *The Navy of the American Revolution*, Cleveland, The Burrows Brothers Co., 1906.

Perna, Rita: *Fashion Forecasting*, New York, Fairchild Publications, 1987.

Rachlis, Eugene: *The Story of the U.S. Coast Guard*, New York, Random House, 1961.

Reis, Ronald A.: *Careers in Art and Graphic Design*, Hauppage, Barrons, 2001.

Rocha, Tony L.: *Careers in Magazine Publishing*, New York, Rosen, 2001.

Rubinstein, Donna: *The Modeling Life*, New York, Berkeley Publishing Group, 1998.

Satterthwaite, Frank: *The Career Portfolio Workbook*, New York, McGraw-Hill, 2003.

Seguin, James: *Media Career Guide*, Boston, St. Martin's, 2006.

Sones, Melissa: *Getting into Fashion: A Career Guide*, New York, Ballantine, 1984.

Vogt, Peter: *Career Opportunities in the Fashion Industry*, New York, Facts on File, 2002.

Wilson, Wayne: *Careers in Publishing and Communications*, Bear, Mitchell Lane, 2002.

Yager, Fred, & Jan Yager: *Career Opportunities in the Film Industry*, New York, Ferguson, 2003.

Zahler, Karen Gantz.: *Superchefs: Signature Recipes From America's New Royalty*, New York, John Wiley & Sons, 1996.

Index

A

B

C

D

E

F

G

H

I

L

M

N

O

P

R

S

T

U

V

W

Y

❑❑❑